Editor:
Jodi L. McClay, M.A.

Project Manager:
Betsy Morris, Ph.D.

Editor in Chief:
Sharon Coan, M.S. Ed.

Art Director:
Elayne Roberts

Art Coordination Assistant:
Cheri Macoubrie Wilson

Cover Artist:
Tina DeLeon

Product Manager:
Phil Garcia

Imaging:
Ralph Olmedo Jr.

Publishers:
Rachelle Cracchiolo, M.S. Ed.
Mary Dupuy Smith, M.S. Ed.

INTEGRATING TECHNOLOGY
into the
Social Studies Curriculum

PRIMARY

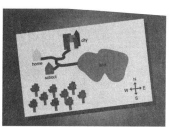

Author:

Fran Clark

Teacher Created Materials, Inc.
6421 Industry Way
Westminster, CA   92683
ISBN-1-57690-430-X

©1998 Teacher Created Materials, Inc.   Made in U.S.A.

TABLE OF CONTENTS

TABLE OF CONTENTS (cont.)

INTRODUCTION

Schools are moving into the Information Age, and the computer is becoming an essential classroom tool and resource. Successful students in the 21st century will need the abilities to think critically, engage in problem solving, and possess interpersonal skills to work effectively in cooperative groups. In addition, they will need to be highly literate and know how to use technology to access and organize information.

Integrating Technology into the Social Studies Curriculum (Primary) is a 144-page resource book that provides strategies and activities for integrating technology skills into the grades 1–3 social studies curriculum. These integrated lessons allow teachers to incorporate computer work into their existing curriculum. After all, what teacher has the time available in the instructional day to add a new subject area? Not only would this be difficult, if not impossible, it would not be in the best interest of students. Research shows that an integrated curriculum is much more valuable. Therefore, the foundation for this book, infusing technology skills into the curriculum, is a more meaningful approach to teaching and learning.

The activities in this book are designed to incorporate computer technology and learning experiences from many disciplines and to place them in the context of the real world. As students work through these activities, they will interact with computers as a part of their everyday classroom experiences and work cooperatively and actively on real-world tasks. Each section contains instructional strategies, a computer application, specific social studies concepts that have been correlated to the National Council of Social Studies standards, related Internet sites, and extended activities.

Prior to the lessons, *Integrating Technology into the Social Studies Curriculum (Primary)* provides information on managing computers in the classroom, whether it be a one-computer classroom, multi-computer classroom, or lab setting. It also includes realistic ways to group students for instruction and practice, as well as positive ways to manage behavior. In addition, successful tips for writing and obtaining grants are discussed.

The book concludes with valuable forms to assist teachers in integrating technology. Samples include computer journal templates, storyboards, databases, self-checking skill sheets, rubrics, and related Web sites.

Enjoy!

THE ONE-COMPUTER CLASSROOM

The one-computer classroom is a challenge for the teacher, but with some planning and thought it is manageable. While lessons can take longer to complete, sometimes days longer than with the use of a lab, teachers in one-computer classrooms can still provide their students with meaningful and enjoyable computer experiences.

Some questions arise when considering the logistics of a one-computer classroom. For example,

- What will the other students do when not on the computer?
- How will the teacher assess each child's progress?
- What kind of system will allow each child a turn?

While these questions are not anything new to teachers, the computer does present some unique situations.

Getting Started

Students will have to be shown how to perform certain operations. These are directions of a physical nature and at times will need to be step-by-step. This means the teacher may have to spend time with individual students until they learn how to click the mouse, click on buttons, or drag and drop objects on the screen. Some planning will be required to ensure that the teacher can work with one or two students while the rest of the class has another task.

An equitable system for students to have time to work on assignments must be planned as well. One of the best methods is to rotate students on a daily basis to do assigned tasks. If a projection device is available, the whole class can work together on some things.

Projection Devices

Projection devices can be expensive but are worth the investment. Since a projection device is not something that teachers use every day, it might be more feasible if several teachers in a school request one that could be shared. A projection device allows the teacher to show the whole class the computer screen at the same time and introduce new material on the computer efficiently with one computer. Students will still need some hands-on time when learning new skills, but with a projection device, the learning curve will be much shorter. Also, many of the lessons in this book can become whole-class activities, especially when introduced or reviewed by using a projection device.

There are several types of projection devices, and they come in a wide range of prices. LCD (liquid crystal display) panels are among the most affordable. They generally start around $1,500 for one with good resolution. They can go up to more than $5,000 for deluxe models. Regardless of the model, LCD panels are simple to use; they fit on top of an overhead projector and connect to the computer. The overhead projects what is on the computer through the LCD panel to a screen in the front of the room. It is important to have an overhead projector that lights up from the base so that its light travels through the LCD panel. Most overheads sold today are made to do this. Older overhead projectors may have their light source in the head that is above the base. This type of overhead will not work with an LCD panel.

THE ONE-COMPUTER CLASSROOM *(cont.)*

Another popular type of projection device is a television that is modified with a translator card and a special cord so that it can translate the computer's digital signal into an analog signal that can be shown by the television. This type of projection device usually costs less than an LCD panel but does not offer the clarity of picture or resolution found with LCD panels.

Projectors are one-piece devices that connect to the computer and then directly project onto the screen. They offer the best looking picture around, but they are also the most costly. Projectors usually start around $5,000.

When looking for the best price, it is best to look in several catalogs. Check with area computer stores and the school librarian for catalogs that feature projection devices. These devices are becoming more affordable as they become more available.

If the computer has not yet been purchased, try to get an oversized monitor and arrange it so that so that the monitor is slightly raised. This will allow a group of students to view the monitor as they sit around the computer table. While this solution is not a projection system, it will help make things a little easier when the teacher is working with a small group around the computer.

Whole-Class Instruction

There are many activities in this book that begin or follow up with a class discussion. As teachers, we know that a great deal can be accomplished by talking with students and modeling the appropriate behavior or skill. Therefore, regardless of the number of computers in the classroom, teachers must utilize traditional intructional practices when teaching technology skills.

Teachers will need to spend time teaching basic skills to students in the beginning, but once students learn these skills, they will become more independent, freeing the teacher to work in other areas of the classroom. Students who use the computer regularly and see teachers using it regularly will develop a higher level of computer literacy, and more quickly, than students who rarely use or see one used.

THE ONE-COMPUTER CLASSROOM *(cont.)*

There are lessons in this resource book that do not even involve the use of a computer, because a lot of the curriculum for computers at the primary level involves teaching students the vocabulary of computers. This means giving them activities that promote intuitive understanding of what the terminology means. Students need to know what is actually happening when they use database software to sort or order records. With intuitive understanding of the functions, they will be able to interpret and use the results of the computer's response more effectively. Lessons like these help young students develop an understanding of computer functions and commands. This helps them become computer literate much faster when they are introduced to more complex software, such as spreadsheets, in the later grades.

Making It Work

Using the computer, talking about the computer, and exploring what can be done with the computer will go a long way toward satisfying almost any primary technology curriculum. It will also provide a sound understanding of the basics of daily computer work that will help students to advance in both technical skills and understanding of concepts as they proceed through the grades.

Teachers do not need a lot of peripherals or a huge computer lab to teach technology skills. One computer with a paint program, multimedia software, and an integrated office package that provides database, spreadsheet, and word processing applications can be the basis for satisfying both the curriculum's technology objectives and the students' needs for the future.

THE MULTI-COMPUTER CLASSROOM

The multi-computer classroom has three or more computers and allows the teacher to work with small groups or the entire class in technology-based activities and to use the computers in many different ways simultaneously.

Grouping Students

In a multi-computer classroom it is necessary to organize the students into cooperative groups so that they can get the most out of computer time. A group of students can be assigned to each computer, where they can research, create projects, publish writing, and save their work. It is important that students are grouped with different abilities, genders, and technology competencies. Also, groups should be switched periodically to provide the students opportunities to work with others in the classroom.

Each member within a group needs to be assigned a specific task for the duration of each activity. These tasks can be put on laminated cards, and students can choose a task card before an activity begins. There are many tasks that can be performed by students. (The teacher should determine which ones are appropriate for each lesson.) Some examples of tasks for computer-based activities are

- Recorder—records group's data
- Cleaner—puts supplies away
- Tracker—makes sure that group members stay on task
- Supplier—gets supplies for group
- Presenter—presents group's findings to class
- Text Writer—inputs text into the computer
- Graphics Artist—inputs graphics items into the computer
- Calculator—performs calculations on the computer
- Graph Maker—makes the computer graph

THE MULTI-COMPUTER CLASSROOM *(cont.)*

It is important to have special rules that apply when students are working in cooperative groups. Each group can make a short list of rules that they will follow when they are working together. Or, perhaps more appropriate for younger children, the teacher can hold a class discussion and decide the special rules that will be needed for group work. Regardless of the method used to determine the rules, they should be written down for all to see. Older students can write the rules on on a piece of paper along with the name of the group's project and each group member's name and assigned task. This piece of paper can be attached to a pocket folder in which each group keeps a disk and all written work related to the project.

Noise Level Control

Many of the activities in the multi-computer classroom are cooperative-learning based. In this environment, the students are encouraged to communicate with each other. A classroom of 25 students can create a lot of noise when they are working on a project. Therefore, it is necessary to have a system of controlling noise. An example that works well is a numerical system, where the 0 signifies "Silence;" a 1 "Quiet;" a 2 "Conversation;" and a 3 "Presentation."

0	Silence	
1	Quiet	☺
2	Conversation	☺ ☺
3	Presentation	☺ ☺ ☺

Laminated cards can be displayed at each computer or in the front of the classroom to indicate the accepted noise level for an activity.

At times, it may be necessary to get everyone's attention quickly. A signal for complete silence could simply be to turn off the classroom lights. This signal tells the students to stop whatever they are doing, look at the teacher, and listen for directions.

THE MULTI-COMPUTER CLASSROOM *(cont.)*

Asking for Help

When working in cooperative groups, students will have questions that many times can be answered by other group members. In fact, it is valuable to teach students other ways of finding answers, besides asking the teacher. For those questions that must be answered by the teacher, one idea is to have students place a brightly colored plastic cup on top of the computer monitor to signal that help is needed.

Equity

Making sure that all students have an opportunity to work on the computer can be difficult. Teachers can make this task easier if they use a visual display to indicate who has or has not been to the computer. There are a variety of ways to record this, but one simple way is to place a laminated square near each computer. Divide the square in half. The left side of the square is designated for those students who have not been to the computer, and the right side is for those students who have.

At the beginning of the week, place a clothespin for each group member on the "Not Been There Yet" side of the square. As the students participate in computer activities, they move their clothespins from the "Not Been There Yet" to the "Been There, Done That" side. When everyone in the group has had a turn, the clothespins are put on the "Not Been There Yet" side of the square again.

THE MULTI-COMPUTER CLASSROOM *(cont.)*

Behavior Management

Due to the nature of the cooperative learning environment, teachers must have clear expectations and specific guidelines for acceptable student behavior in the multi-computer classroom. The teacher may want students to do some role playing exercises to reinforce acceptable classroom behavior. Students can help in generating these rules. The teacher may even want students to participate in choosing logical consequences for poor behavior choices. Below are some rules that are appropriate for a primary multi-computer classroom.

RULES

1. Enter quietly and ready to listen.
2. Respect your work and the work of others.
3. Treat the equipment with respect.
4. Listen carefully and follow directions.
5. Clean up your area and exit quietly

Computer Journals

It is helpful for each student to keep a computer journal. Students can make entries in their journals at the end of each activity. They can explain what they have learned about the subject, describe what they did on the computer, and list any problems they had using the computer or working within their group. The teacher should review the journals to track student progress, address student problems, and evaluate what the students have learned during each activity.

THE COMPUTER LAB

The ideal situation for schools is to have a computer lab equipped with enough computers for every student in a class, as well as computers in each classroom for students to work on when not in the lab. The downfall of a lab setting is that students only visit it periodically (perhaps once a week) and thereby lose practice and daily experiences with technology. Therefore, having a few computers in each classroom, in addition to a school lab, is the most beneficial for all.

Lab Schedules

In most schools with a lab setting, each class is assigned one class period per week to work in the computer lab. Teachers may decide that for one week one teacher will bring both classes to the computer lab and vice versa. This allows each classroom teacher the option of either teaching the lesson, having the paired teacher teach it for both classes, or having the technology lab specialist teach the lesson (if one is available).

An important thing to remember is that activities in the computer lab must be curriculum related. The lab should not be free time to play games or just draw pictures! Students should be given instruction and work on an activity or project that relates to what they are studying in class.

It is helpful when scheduling lab lessons to leave a regular block of time or day of the week when the lab is free. That way, teachers can schedule an extra period for the entire class or group of students. (This is particularly helpful when long-term projects are being developed.)

Assigned Seats

A seating chart is extremely important for the lab setting, as students are in a different setting and tend to become excited and therefore noisy. A permanent, assigned seat will help students focus on the task at hand and realize that the goal is to work in the lab, not to socialize with friends.

COMPUTER LAB SCHEDULE

Monday May 4, 1998

Time	Teacher	Subject	Objective	Software	Technology Specialist Needed for
8:05–9:00	Teacher A			ClarisWorks Kid Pix 2 SuperPrint HyperStudio Internet Other	Instruction Support Home
9:00–9:45	Teacher B			ClarisWorks Kid Pix 2 SuperPrint HyperStudio Internet Other	Instruction Support Home
9:45–10:30	Teacher C			ClarisWorks Kid Pix 2 SuperPrint HyperStudio Internet Other	Instruction Support Home
10:30–11:15	Teacher D			ClarisWorks Kid Pix 2 SuperPrint HyperStudio Internet Other	Instruction Support Home
11:15–12:00	Teacher E			ClarisWorks Kid Pix 2 SuperPrint HyperStudio Internet Other	Instruction Support Home
12:00–12:45	Teacher F			ClarisWorks Kid Pix 2 SuperPrint HyperStudio Internet Other	Instruction Support Home
12:45–1:30	Teacher G			ClarisWorks Kid Pix 2 SuperPrint HyperStudio Internet Other	Instruction Support Home
1:30–2:15	Teacher H			ClarisWorks Kid Pix 2 SuperPrint HyperStudio Internet Other	Instruction Support Home

COMPUTER LAB LAYOUT

Even Printer

Odd Printer

Large Screen Monitor

Teacher's Desk

Teacher's Name

Door

WRITING A GRANT

Everyone uses technology, right? Maybe, but how much, how often, and why? The answers to these questions are determined by the big, bad budget! Technology capabilities of schools vary. Some schools are equipped with a full computer lab of 30 up-to-the-minute computers, many color printers, scanners, digital cameras, LCD panels for viewing—you name it, the works! These schools might also have several computer stations in each classroom, again fully equipped. On the other end of the spectrum are schools that might have a computer station available for two or three classrooms to share. Whatever the situation, we all want more! We have begged our PTAs, who continually do whatever they can for our children's needs. Some schools have built business partnerships in their communities. However, an often overlooked possibility is that of grant writing. And yes! There is suport out there. We just have to know how to get it. Before even starting, enlist the help of others on the staff, possibly creating a technology grant task force because it is always better to brainstorm with others on projects this important.

Who?

Begin with your school district. Many districts give small grants to teachers or teams of teachers for specific needs. They may offer stipends for projects developed that will enhance teaching and learning. Usually, these projects need to help more than one class and can be replicated and made available to other teachers.

Next, seek out a community foundation which funds projects just in your county. Often, an RFP (request for proposal) is accepted quarterly or annually.

Many corporations are searching for places to put their money. Why? Besides helping schools, awarding grants is a big tax deduction. If these corporations do not find ways to deduct profits, of course, Uncle Sam gets them.

And speaking of Uncle Sam, the government also gives grants. There are both state and national grant opportunities!

Where?

Most libraries will have an index to help locate national and state grants. Corporations like Kodak and Coca-cola are also good sources. The Internet is a wonderful source for addresses of grant makers, and most libraries have Internet access. Here are two tips when searching the Net: be specific and accurate, and try *grants+technology* to connect two words for the search engines.

WRITING A GRANT *(cont.)*

What?

Now that you know who gives grants and where these resources are located, you need tips on writing.

State the Problem

You cannot simply ask for money. You must identify a need that can be connected with technology. For example, in order to motivate third graders and increase their reading scores, the students will create multimedia presentations after researching science topics such as earth/moon cycles, the food chain, and animal habitats.

Write the Plan

Be very specific. Using the example above, state exactly how you plan to improve reading scores with this strategy. For example, "the students will each choose an animal, read many books about the animal, take notes while researching, and write paragraphs on the computer about the main topics. The students will create multimedia slide shows with the information garnered. They will include clipart and scanned pieces from student drawings. The motivation generated by being able to use these hands-on materials will encourage students' reading, increase vocabulary, demonstrate improved synthesizing, and much more."

Prove It

Those who review grant proposals want hard evidence that you will attempt to measure the outcome of the plan. Include proof that technology can help solve the problem. For example, state that seventy per cent of the third-grade students will show at least a four-point improvement in their reading scores. The entire faculty will receive staff development training in the use of the hardware and software necessary to achieve these goals.

Determine a Time Line

Tell how long the project will take. For instance, "staff development will begin in September and be successfully completed in eight weeks. Students will begin work at multimedia work stations by November, and their slide shows will be completed by February. They will share their slide shows with parents at an open house and with other classrooms after the PTA Open House. These students will then become tutors for students the following year."

Research the Budget

It is extremely important to itemize absolutely everything you need for the project, including personnel for training, stipends for staff development, and all hardware and software. This is where you demonstrate the research that goes into your grant. If continuing funds are necessary, you need to stipulate where you will get those funds.

WRITING A GRANT *(cont.)*

How?

It takes some thought and practice to match the project with the right funding source. You will need to carefully read the RFP (request for proposal) and follow all instructions exactly. If others in your district have responded to RFPs previously, you may want to use their documents as a model. Check with your district office to see what is available before "reinventing the wheel."

Success!

It is very unusual for a first-time grant writer to achieve success. Don't become discouraged. A "no" may really mean "not at this time." If you are fortunate enough to meet success the first time, you will most likely be energized to try for an even bigger grant. If you were told that your grant was a good one but not selected at this time, try again with a different funder. Look over the RFP carefully, and submit it again. Go back to your team for more brainstorming. Perhaps your budget needs review, or maybe some items can be eliminated or postponed for later.

For further information on grant writing, see Teacher Created Materials' *Writing Grants* by Julia Jasmine.

Good luck ... there's lots of money out there. Go get it!

WHAT EVERY HOME NEEDS ... A DATABASE ACTIVITY

A home needs certain things to be a good place to live. For example, homes need beds for sleeping and windows for sunlight. Do they need a TV in every room? What about a microwave?

Grades: 2–3

Duration: 40 minutes

Instructional Objective: Students will categorize given examples of household items into those that are needs and those that are wants. Then they will enter data into a simple database template.

Materials: teacher-created database template, page 19; copies of item cards and think sheets, pages 20 and 21

Computer Software: *ClarisWorks* or *Microsoft Word*

Procedure:

Before the Computer:

Ask the students to imagine that they are moving into an empty house and can only bring one thing from their old houses. Discuss the concept of needs vs. wants. Have them discuss what they would bring and why, and record their ideas on the Home Sweet Home Think Sheet on page 21.

On the Computer:

Put the students into cooperative groups of four. Assign each group the following tasks: card reader, presenter, recorder, and computer operator. Give each group the set of home item cards on page 20. Tell the students that the card reader will read each card. The group will need to decide if the item is absolutely necessary (a need) or if they could live without it (a want). The computer operator will enter the name of the item on the database template and either yes (if the item is absolutely necessary) or no (we could live without it). After the data has been entered, the computer operator will sort the data to list those things that are needs and those that are wants. The recorder will record the group's results on the Home Sweet Home Think Sheet on page 21.

After the Computer:

The presenter will present the group's results. The teacher should host a discussion as to why certain items are needs and why others are wants.

Extended Activity:

Have students cut pictures from magazines and catalogs to make a poster that illustrates "What Every Home Needs."

HOME SWEET HOME DATABASE

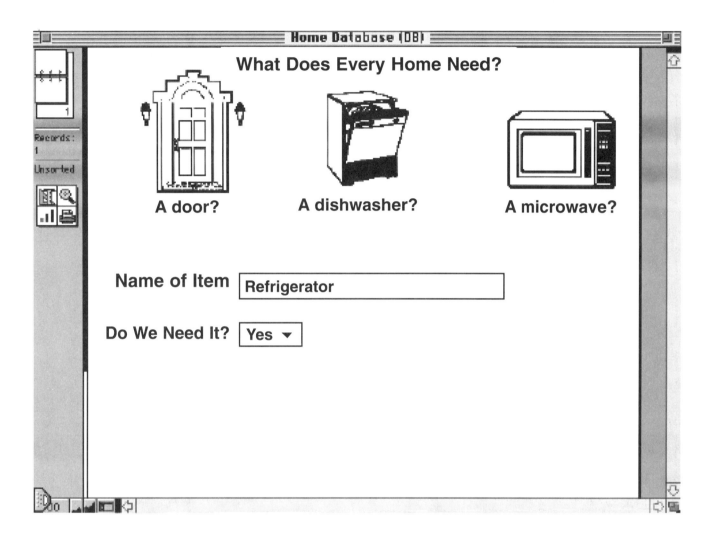

HOME SWEET HOME ITEM CARDS

Stove   Microwave   Shower

Television   Sink   Refrigerator

Clock   Swimming Pool   Lamp

Table   Telephone   Computer

HOME SWEET HOME THINK SHEET

Group Members: _____ Date _____

Quick Talk

Pretend that you are moving into a new house. You can only bring one item with you. What would it be and why? _____

_____

Data Collection

Our list of items that are absolutely necessary (needs): _____

_____

Our list of items that we could live without (wants): _____

_____

Reflection

What have you learned about needs and wants?

A need is _____

A want is _____

MY HOME SURVEY ... A DATABASE ACTIVITY

Most of us spend a lot of time at home. We know our homes well. Or, do we? Do you know how many windows and doors are in your home? How many feet wide is your bedroom?

Grades: 2–3

Duration: three 30–40 minute sessions

Instructional Objective: The students will record details about a home, enter data into a database template, and search a database to answer questions about homes.

Materials: teacher-created database template, page 24; copies of data collection and think sheets, pages 23 and 25

Computer Software: *Inspiration, ClarisWorks, Microsoft Word*

Procedure:

Before the Computer:

Discuss why shelter is one of our three basic needs. Use a program such as *Inspiration* to make a concept web. It will clarify what things are important about shelter, no matter where it is, how it looks, or how many people live in it. Have students brainstorm the parts and details that make up a home, such as doors, windows, color, etc. Explain that all homes are different and that each home has many different parts and details.

Explain that before students can work on a computer database, they will need to survey their homes and complete the "My Home Survey" on page 23 for homework.

On the Computer:

The next day, lead a discussion about the results of the "My Home Surveys." Using page 24 as a sample, the teacher and students should create a "My Home Survey" database template. Elicit the fields for the database by asking the students to name the parts of a home, such as doors, and details, such as color. Have each student enter the data from his or her survey into the class database. Then, demonstrate how to perform a database search.

After the Computer:

Divide the students into groups of four. Have them search the "My Home Database" to answer questions on the "My Home Survey Think Sheet" on page 25.

Extended Activity:

Make a house book. Write a definition and draw an illustration for words that have "house" in them. Use words such as doghouse, birdhouse, houseboat, playhouse, lighthouse, White House, dollhouse, tree house. Discuss why some of the words are compound words and some are not.

MY HOME SURVEY

Name _____   Date _____

Detail	Yes/No	Color/Material	Number
Windows			
Doors			
Stories			
Porch			
Roof			
Fireplace			
Shutters			

Most of us spend a lot of time at home, but do we really know the details of our home? Explore your home and complete the survey above.

MY HOME DATABASE

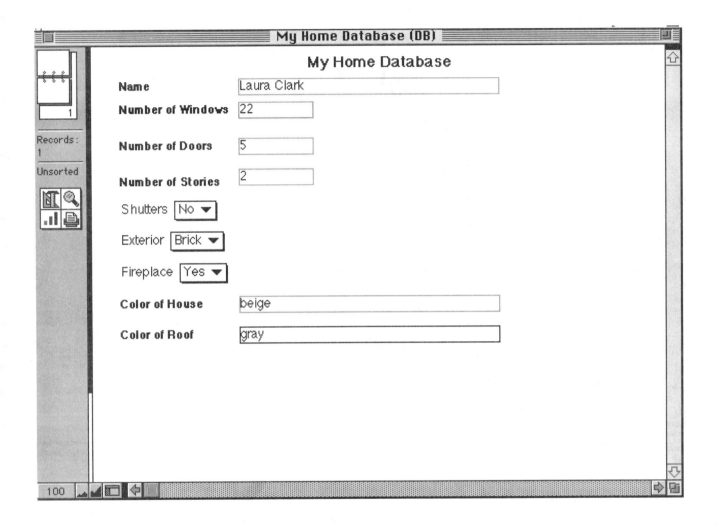

MY HOME SURVEY THINK SHEET

Name _____ Date _____

Quick Talk

What makes your home a shelter? Discuss it with your group and write down your ideas. _____

_____

Data Manipulation

1. Whose home has the greatest number of windows? _____

2. Whose home has the least number of windows? _____

3. Whose homes have the same number of windows? _____

4. How many people's homes have a fireplace? _____

5. How many people's homes have shutters? _____

6. How many people live in a one–story home? _____

7. How many people live in a two–story home? _____

8. Does anyone live in a green home? _____

9. How many people live in a home made of wood? _____

10. Who in your group has a home most like yours? Why? _____

Reflection

Write a sentence to tell something that you have learned about homes.

_____

_____

YOUR DREAM BEDROOM ... A DRAWING ACTIVITY

People use floor plans to show the placement of furniture and other details in a room. Imagine that you have just won a contest and the prize is a brand new dream bedroom. You may have whatever you want, no matter what it costs. What would your dream bedroom look like?

Grades: 2–3

Duration: 30 minutes

Instructional Objective: The students will design an imaginary room and produce a computer generated floor plan.

Materials: teacher-created floor plan template, page 27; copies of activity sheet, page 28

Computer Software: *ClarisWorks, Microsoft Works, Kid Pix*

Procedure:

Before the Computer:

Explain that floor plans are used by architects, interior designers, and builders to show the placement of elements such as doors, windows, and closets in a room. Compare a floor plan to a map. Point out that a map and a floor plan are drawings that show places and that these places are seen as if one is looking down upon them. Floor plans show the location of windows, doors, furniture, and other room elements in relation to each other. Discuss when and for whom a floor plan would be useful.

On the Computer:

Have the students work individually at the computer, using a computer-generated floor plan template and directions sheet to make floor plans of their dream bedrooms.

After the Computer:

Have the students orally share their dream bedroom floor plans. Students can illustrate their dream bedrooms for a classroom bulletin board display.

Internet Link:

Snurry's Burrow—a floor plan of a little rabbit's burrow *http://wwwWeblynx.com.au/snurry.htm*

Extended Activities:

1. Write a short, descriptive paragraph entitled "My Dream Bedroom."

2. Make a shoebox diorama of "My Dream Bedroom."

3. Make a picture book of bedrooms, for example, an astronaut's bedroom on a spaceship, a princess's bedroom in a castle, or a cowboy's bedroom on a ranch.

DREAM BEDROOM FLOOR PLAN TEMPLATE

Note: Have the students use this template to make the floor plans of their dream bedrooms. They can add other symbols if so desired. This template needs to be made by the teacher and saved as a stationery file. Put this template file on the computer before the students begin.

A floor plan is like a map of a room. Symbols show where windows, doors, and furniture are located. Make a floor plan of your dream bedroom. Use the symbols in the key below.

_____'s Dream Bedroom Floor Plan

Key:

Window   bed   chair   desk   TV   door

MY DREAM BEDROOM FLOOR PLAN DIRECTIONS

A floor plan is like a map of a room. Symbols show where windows, doors, and furniture are located. Make a floor plan of your dream bedroom. Use the symbols in the key below.

Key:

window	bed	chair	desk	TV	door

rectangle   oval   rounded rectangle   line

1. Use the ⬛ to make the window, bed, and desk.

2. Use the ⬭ to make the chair.

3. Use the ⬜ to make the TV.

4. Use the ╲ to make the door.

5. Print your dream bedroom floor plan.

6. Write your name on your paper.

WHITE HOUSE PETS ... A SPREADSHEET ACTIVITY

Presidents and their families have had many pets live with them in the White House. President John F. Kennedy's daughter had a pet named Macaroni. Can you guess what kind of pet Macaroni was?

Grades: 2–3

Duration: 60 minutes

Instructional Objective: The students will search a Web page for information and record it on the collection sheet on page 30. They will use the data to create simple spreadsheets and charts.

Materials: copies of data collection and think sheets, pages 30 and 32; spreadsheet directions sheet, page 31; Internet connection

Computer Software: *ClarisWorks, Microsoft Works, Netscape Navigator*

Procedure:

Before the Computer:

Ask students who lives in the White House. Besides the First Family, discuss their pets and what it might be like for them to live in the White House. Ask if any students have ever visited the White House. Using the Internet link listed below, take the class on a virtual tour of the White House led by Socks, the Clinton family's cat. Explain that other presidents have also had pets and brainstorm a list of the kinds of pets that could live in the White House.

On the Computer:

Have students work with partners to learn about the kids and their pets who have lived in the White House. Have them explore the White House for Kids home page and record the kind and number of pets that the children have had. Finally, have them use the data to create spreadsheets and charts.

After the Computer:

Have the students share their charts and tell interesting facts about pets in the White House.

Internet Links:

The White House for Kids—a kid's tour of the White House
http://www.whitehouse.gov/WH/Kids/html/home.html
Electronic Zoo—animal-related Net resources
http://netvet.wustl.edu/e-zoo.htm

Extended Activities:

1. Draw a White House pet and write an interesting fact about it.

2. Take a class pet survey and create a bar graph to show the kinds and numbers of pets owned by classmates.

3. Make a class book entitled "Our Pets."

4. Write the directions for the care and feeding of a family pet.

WHITE HOUSE PETS DATA COLLECTION SHEET

Click on the blue star numbered 5.

Look at the photographs and read the information. For more White House pets, scroll to the bottom of the page and click More.

Record the name of each kind of pet found. Keep a tally of the number of each kind of pet in the box below:

Pet	Number

WHITE HOUSE PETS SPREADSHEET DIRECTIONS

Use data from the data collection sheet to create this spreadsheet and graph.

Open the Spreadsheet application. Under file menu click on New.

	A	B	C
1	Pet	Number	
2			
3			
4			
5			

Enter the data in the spreadsheet.

Drag the cursor over the data.

	A	B	C
1	Pet	Number	
2			
3			
4			
5			

Go to the Options menu and click Make Chart.

Choose Chart and click OK.

Print your chart.

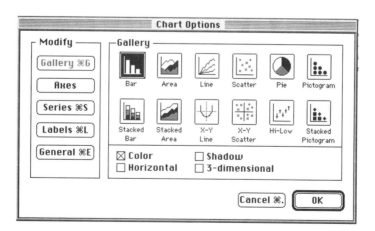

WHITE HOUSE PETS THINK SHEET

Name _____ Date _____

What kind of pet do you think Macaroni was?

Write an interesting fact that you learned about pets in the White House.

_____

What pet(s) did the kids who lived in the White House have most?

_____

What pet(s) did the kids who lived in the White House have least?

_____

What pet was the most unusual?

_____

If we surveyed this class, what pet do you think would be most popular and why?

_____

What do you think would be the best kind of pet to live in the White House and why?

_____

ON THE STREET WHERE I LIVE ... A MAP DRAWING ACTIVITY

Where do you live? Do you live in a city, a town, or the country? Make a street map to show where you live!

Grades: 1–3

Duration: 60 minutes

Instructional Objective: The students will use a street map to investigate a neighborhood and the paint/draw application to draw a simple street map.

Materials: teacher-created computer template, page 34; Internet connection

Computer Software: *ClarisWorks, Microsoft Works, Netscape Navigator, Internet Explorer*

Procedure:

Before the Computer:

Ask the students to compare and contrast a city, a town, and the country. Ask them to describe where they live. Discuss whether they live in a city, a town, or the country. What kind of homes would be found in each of these areas?

On the Computer:

Have the students work with partners to explore street maps and use the Internet Web site: *Mapquest* to view street maps of their neighborhoods. After they explore their neighborhood street maps, have them use a teacher-created template, as on page 34, to make a simple map of their street.

After the Computer:

Have the students share their maps and tell something that they like about living in their neighborhood. Students can also write why they think their homes are special, using the writing template on page 35.

Internet Links:

Mapquest—an interactive atlas that allows you to find virtually any street address *http://wwwmapquest.com*

Mapmaker, Mapmaker, Make Me a Map—the history of mapmaking and a description of how maps are made *http://loki.ur.utk.edu/ut2Kids/maps/map.html*

Extended Activities:

1. Make a classroom book entitled "Our Street Map Book."

2. Draw a map for the school's street.

3. Explore an atlas.

ON THE STREET WHERE I LIVE TEMPLATE

Write the name of your street on the street sign.

Use the drawing tools to draw a picture to show what kind of house you live in.

Write your house number on it.

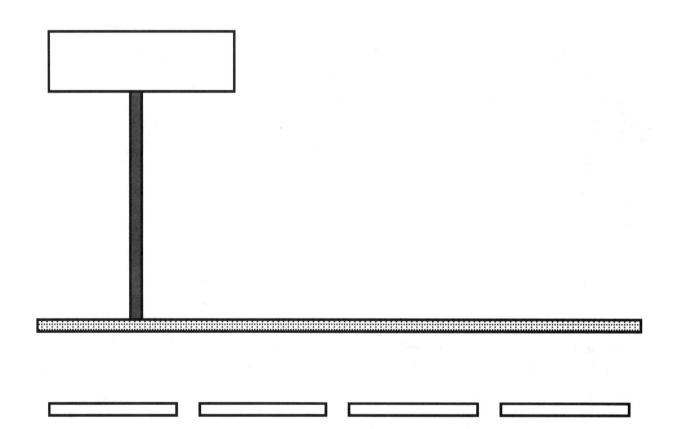

Note: This template needs to be made by the teacher and saved as a stationery file on the computer before the students begin.

WRITING TEMPLATE

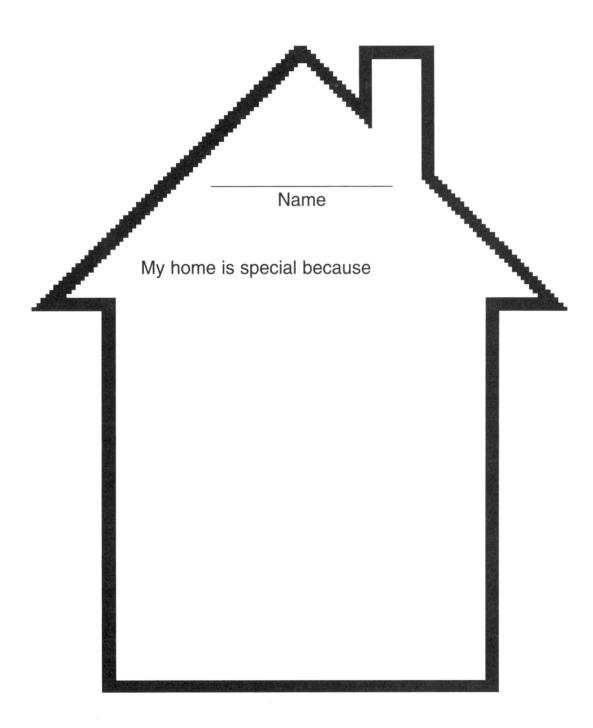

_____

Name

My home is special because

Note: The students can each use this template to write a short paragraph about what makes their house special. This template needs to be made by the teacher and saved as a stationery file on the computer before the students begin. Have the students cut out their houses and put them together to make a classroom book.

A FAMILY HISTORY QUILT ... A DRAWING ACTIVITY

In the mid-19th century quilts were made to mark a special occasion. You can make a paper quilt to mark the special events that have occurred in your family. Each square represents a special event in your family's history.

Grades: 2–3

Duration: 30 minutes

Instructional Objective: The students will use a paint/draw program to make a family history quilt. They will use pieces of clip art to symbolize special family events.

Materials: teacher-created computer template, page 37; clipart

Computer Software: *ClarisWorks* or *Microsoft Works*

Procedure:

Before the Computer:

Discuss where quilt pieces come from. Emphasize that different pieces of quilts sometimes come from a family's old clothing, and a quilt can become a piece of family history. Show examples of different quilt designs.

On the Computer:

Each student will design a quilt that represents his or her family history.

After the Computer:

Have students share their quilts and tell about special events that have occurred in their families.

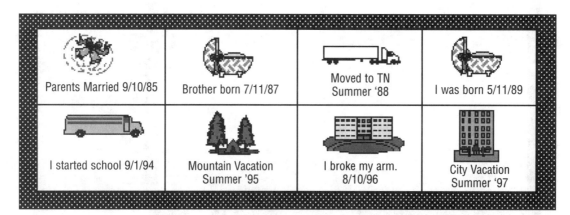

Extended Activities:

1. Make individual student quilts. Students can cut pictures from magazines and catalogs that tell about them. For example, a picture of a soccer ball could represent that a student plays on a soccer team.

2. Look up quilts on a CD-ROM encyclopedia. Try to find examples of different quilt patterns.

FAMILY QUILT DIRECTIONS

1. Use the rectangle tool to draw a 10" x 7" inch (25 cm x 18 cm) rectangle. Fill the rectangle with texture or color.

2. Use the rectangle tool to draw a 9" x 6" inch (23 cm x 15 cm) rectangle. Fill the rectangle with white or color.

3. Use the line tool to draw lines to make the quilt squares.

4. Place a piece of clip art in each square to symbolize a special event.

5. Make a text box for each square and put the date that the special event occurred.

Some ideas for special events are weddings, births, family vacations, family reunions, special awards, beginning school, family moves, or a hospital stay.

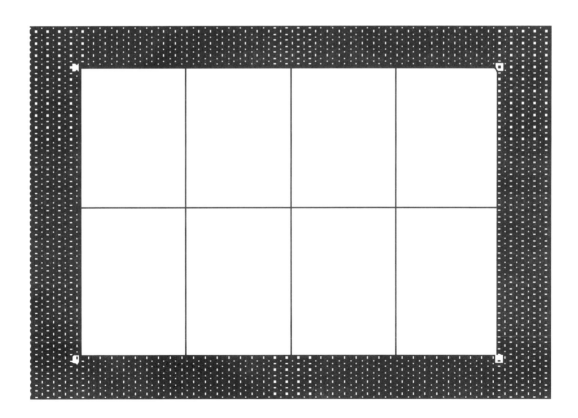

Note: This template needs to be made by the teacher and saved as a stationery file on the computer before the students begin.

A FAMILY FACTS SURVEY ... A SPREADSHEET ACTIVITY

Do you know what a typical family in your classroom is? Do most of your classmates have siblings? Conduct a "Family Facts" survey to discover what makes up the typical family in your classroom.

Grades: 2–3

Duration: two 30-45 minute sessions

Instructional Objective: The students will create and conduct a survey to collect data about their families. Students will enter this data into spreadsheets and then analyze and graph the data to determine what makes up the typical family in their classroom. Students should understand that although family structures may be different, families share some common features.

Materials: copies of student survey, page 44; computer directions, pages 39 and 40

Computer Software: *ClarisWorks* or *Microsoft Works*

Procedure:

Before the Computer:

On Day 1 discuss what a family is. Have the students brainstorm questions about families that will result in a numerical answer. For example, how many sisters do you have? Create a survey form like the sample on page 44 to record the data. Have students conduct the survey with their family members and return their work the following day.

On Day 2 discuss how the collected data can be displayed. Show the students how to enter data into a spreadsheet and make a chart. Discuss the different ways that data can be graphed.

On the Computer:

Have the students work with partners to enter data into a spreadsheet. Each pair of students should be responsible for entering the data for one survey question. After the data has been entered, have the students create a graph. These graphs can be printed and displayed on a classroom bulletin board.

After the Computer:

Discuss the results of the survey. Help students discover what the typical family in their classroom is.

Internet Link:

Find classes in different areas of the country (via the Internet) willing to conduct the "Family Facts" survey in their classrooms. Compare and contrast their data with the class data. What are their typical families like? Are there things that are common to all families no matter where they live?

Extended Activity:

Make a classroom book entitled "A Family Is..." Have each student write and illustrate one page of the book.

A FAMILY FACTS SURVEY DIRECTIONS

1. Create a survey form. Some sample questions:

   - How many people do you live with?
   - How many children does your family have?
   - How many pets does your family have?
   - How many times have you moved since you were born?
   - How many years have you lived in the home where you live now?
   - How old is your oldest living relative?
   - How old is your youngest relative?
   - How many grandparents do you have?
   - How many aunts do you have?
   - How many uncles do you have?
   - How many cousins do you have?

2. Make a tally sheet to record survey data.

	A	**B**	**C**	**D**	**E**	**F**	**G**	**H**	**I**	**J**	**K**	**L**
1	**Question**	0	1	2	3	4	5	6	7	8	9	10
2	How many people do you live with?											
3	How many children does your family have?											
4	How many pets does your family have?											
5	How old is your oldest living relative?											
6	How many uncles do you have?											
7	How many cousins do you have?											

A FAMILY FACTS SURVEY DIRECTIONS

3. Create a spreadsheet for each survey question. Enter data from the tally sheet.

	A	B
1	Student Names	Number of Children
2	Bobby	3
3	Susie	2
4	Billy	1
5	Mary	6
6	Tommy	4
7		
8		
9		
10		
11		

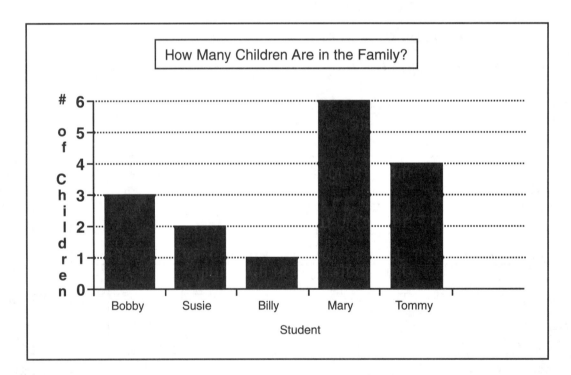

4. Print graphs. Use graphs to analyze what makes up the typical family in your classroom. Discuss how families are similar and how families are different.

5. Display graphs on a bulletin board entitled "All Kinds of Families."

FAMILY FACTS SURVEY

Please complete this form and return it to school by: _____

Name _____ Date _____

Directions: Families are made up of people who share their lives with each other. Tell how many different members are in your family.

1. I live with _____ adults.

2. I have _____ younger sister(s) in my family.

3. I have _____ older sister(s) in my family.

4. I have _____ younger brother(s) in my family.

5. I have _____ older brothers(s) in my family.

6. I have _____ children in my family.

7. I have _____ grandparent(s) in my family.

8. I have _____ aunt(s) in my family.

9. I have _____ uncle(s) in my family.

10. I have _____ cousin(s) in my family.

Here is a picture of my family.

SNAPSHOT BOOK ... A PAINTING AND WRITING ACTIVITY

Every family has a history. Have you ever wondered what it was like to be a child when your grandparents were growing up? Interview a grandparent or an older family member to find out what it was like growing up in another time period.

Grades: 1–3

Duration: 60 minutes

Instructional Objective: The students will each interview a grandparent or an older family member to find out what it was like to be a child growing up in another time period.

Materials: interview questions (either teacher-made or duplicated from page 44), construction paper, scissors

Computer Software: *ClarisWorks, Microsoft Word, Kid Pix*

Procedure:

Before the Computer:

Lead a discussion about what it might be like to be a child who lived in the past. How would a grandparent's childhood be similar or different from students'? Tell students that they will interview a grandparent or an older adult to find out what it was like to be a child in another time period. Discuss what kind of questions students can ask to find out about what it was like.

On the Computer:

Have the students each use the paint/draw application to create a portrait of their grandparent or older family member.

After the Computer:

Have the students print the portrait and then cut it out and glue it in the center of a classroom Snapshot Book, using the directions on the following page. Students will lift up each flap and write a word or phrase that answers an interview question. These books can be displayed on a classroom bulletin board.

Internet Link:

If the student is unable to interview the grandparent or older family member in person, he or she could e-mail the interview questions and ask that the responses be e-mailed back.

Extended Activities:

1. Invite an older adult from the community to talk about what the community was like when he or she was a child.

2. Write "Patchwork Stories" using the master on page 45.

SNAPSHOT BOOK DIRECTIONS

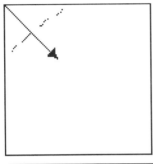

1. Start with an 8 1/2 by 8 1/2 square of construction paper. Fold down each corner to the center of the paper.

2. At each point, cut to the folded edge of the paper.

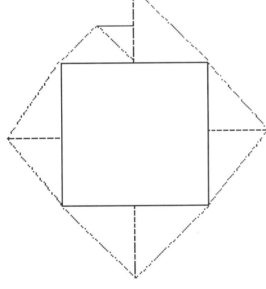

3. Fold down each point so that the tip touches the folded edge of the paper. Crease and cut off. Then fold over at the edge of the paper and crease.

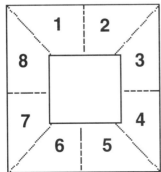

4. Lift up each flap and write a word or phrase that answers an interview question.

INTERVIEW QUESTIONS

Interview a grandparent or special adult family member by asking the following questions. Record the answers on the lines below the questions.

Name of Person Interviewed: _____

Where were you born?

_____

_____

Where did you live when you were growing up?

_____

_____

Do you have any brothers or sisters?

_____

_____

What kind of chores did you do as a child?

_____

_____

What was school like for you?

_____

_____

What did you do for fun when you were my age?

_____

_____

What would you like people to know about your life?

_____

_____

What is the most exciting thing that has ever happened to you?

_____

_____

MY PATCHWORK STORY

Use the answers to the interview questions to write sentences about your grandparent or special family member. Write one sentence for each patch. Write the name of the person you interviewed in the rectangle.

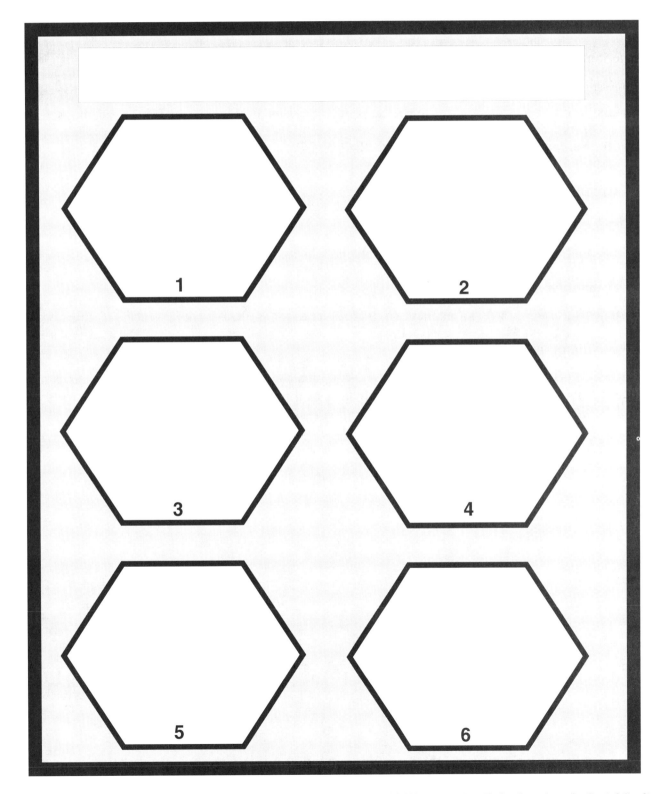

FAMILY TREE ... AN ART ACTIVITY

Every family has a history. A family tree can represent the generations of a family. Make a family tree to show the generations in your family.

Grades: 1–3

Duration: 60 minutes

Instructional Objective: The students will research their family histories to find out the birth dates of their family members. They will use this information to create a family tree.

Materials: teacher-created computer template, page 48; copies of "My Family Tree," page 47; scissors

Computer Software: *ClarisWorks, Microsoft Word, Kid Pix*

Procedure:

Before the Computer:

Explain that a family tree is one way to record the people who make up a family.

On the Computer:

Have students use the paint/draw application to create portraits of their family members.

After the Computer:

Have students print their family member portraits and then cut them out and glue them on their family trees. Students should write the names and birth dates of the family members on their family trees. These family trees can be displayed on a classroom bulletin board.

Extended Activity:

Students can research what countries their family members came from.

MY FAMILY TREE

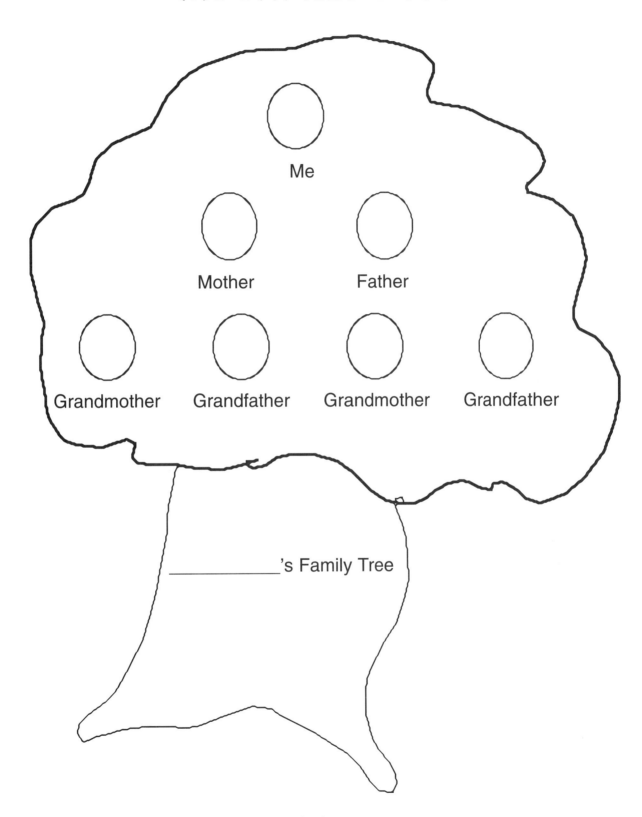

Me

Mother   Father

Grandmother   Grandfather   Grandmother   Grandfather

_____'s Family Tree

Note: Have the students add frames for siblings in the top row.

MY FAMILY TREE

Family Portraits Template

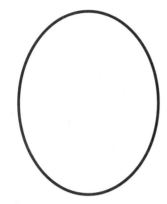

My Name: Birth:

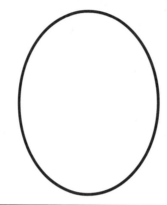

Father's Name: Birth:

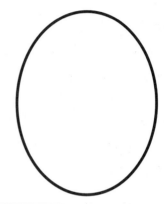

Mother's Name: Birth:

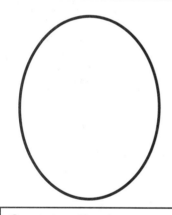

Grandmother's Name: Birth:

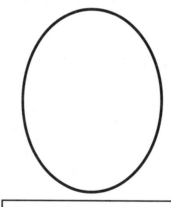

Grandmother's Name: Birth:

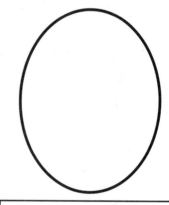

Grandmother's Name: Birth:

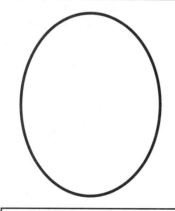

Grandfather's Name: Birth:

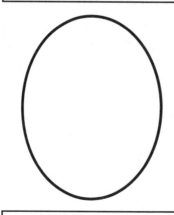

Name: Birth:

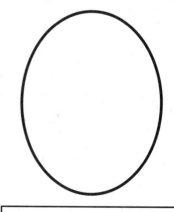

Name: Birth:

A FAMILY TIME LINE

A time line is a way to organize and present facts and dates in chronological order. You can make a family time line to display special events that have occurred in your family.

Grades: 2–3

Duration: Two 30-minute sessions

Instructional Objective: The students will talk with family members and collect eight dates for a family time line. Students will create a family time line and put these dates in chronological order.

Materials: teacher-created computer template, page 51; copies of data collection sheet, page 50; cash register tape; string; scissors

Computer Software: *ClarisWorks, Microsoft Word*

Before the Computer:

Explain that a time line is a way to organize events and dates visually and in sequential order. Review the concept of a number time line. Emphasize that a time line is similar to a number line but that the numbers on a time line are dates. Model a time line using important events from your life. Have the students brainstorm a list of special events that could be displayed on a family time line. Some examples include

- when parents got married
- when children were born
- when the family moved

Ask the students to talk to family members about important events that have occurred in the family and record these events on the data collection sheet.

On the Computer:

Have each student enter his or her special events on the time line template and print one copy.

After the Computer:

Use adding machine tape to make the time line and the event cards as labels for the special family events. Have the students write dates in two-year increments on their pieces of adding machine tape. The students may need help in setting the beginning date and placing event cards that fall between two years on the time line. The beginning date should be based on the dates that the student has collected. Have the students attach the event cards in chronological order (with string) to the time line. Place the time lines around the room. Have the students compare and contrast their family time lines.

Extended Activities:

1. Make a class time line and record special events as they happen throughout the year.

2. Read a biography or autobiography and make a time line of the person's life.

3. Research the space program and make a time line showing the history of the space program.

A FAMILY TIME LINE DATA COLLECTION SHEET

Directions: Ask family members about important events that have occurred in your family. Write about the events in the boxes below.

O
Event 1: _____
_____
_____
_____

O
Event 2: _____
_____
_____
_____

O
Event 3: _____
_____
_____
_____

O
Event 4: _____
_____
_____
_____

O
Event 5: _____
_____
_____
_____

O
Event 6: _____
_____
_____
_____

O
Event 7: _____
_____
_____
_____

O
Event 8: _____
_____
_____
_____

A FAMILY TIME LINE DATA COMPUTER TEMPLATE

Note: This template needs to be made by the teacher and saved as a stationery file. Put this template file on the computer before the students begin.

Directions: Place your cursor after the event and begin typing the information from your data collection sheet. Cut out the event cards and attach them to your time line with a piece of string.

O	O
Event 1:	**Event 2:**

O	O
Event 3:	**Event 4:**

O	O
Event 5:	**Event 6:**

O	O
Event 7:	**Event 8:**

MY FAMILY ... A HYPERSTUDIO PROJECT

Grades: 1–3

Duration: five 30-minute sessions

Instructional Objective: The students will create a six-card *HyperStudio* stack to describe their families.

Materials: copies of storyboards, pages 53 and 54; teacher-created computer templates, pages 55 and 56; computer disks

Computer Software: *HyperStudio*

Before the Computer:

Have the students create a six-card *HyperStudio* stack on the "My Family" storyboards.

On the Computer:

Have students transfer data from their storyboards to the *HyperStudio* Project Computer Template. The students should complete the sentences and use the draw tools to draw illustrations.

After the Computer:

Have the students share stacks on presentation screen or print out their storyboards.

Extended Activities:

1. Students can read and record text for their "My Family" *HyperStudio* stacks.

2. Link students' "My Family" *HyperStudio* stacks together with a table of contents card. This makes it easy for students and parents to explore the stacks, and it becomes a great display for a Parents Open House.

MY FAMILY ... A HYPERSTUDIO PROJECT STORYBOARD

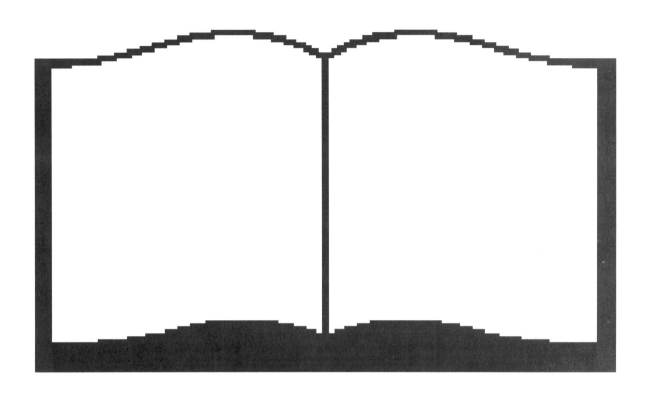

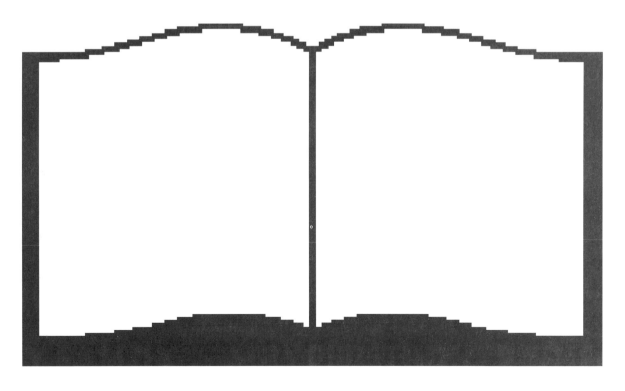

MY FAMILY ... A HYPERSTUDIO PROJECT
STORYBOARD *(cont.)*

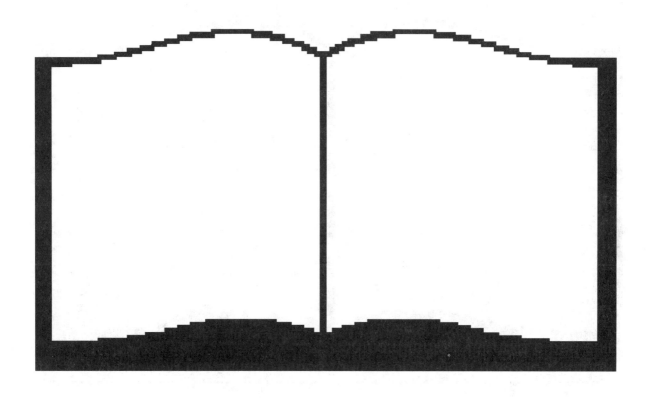

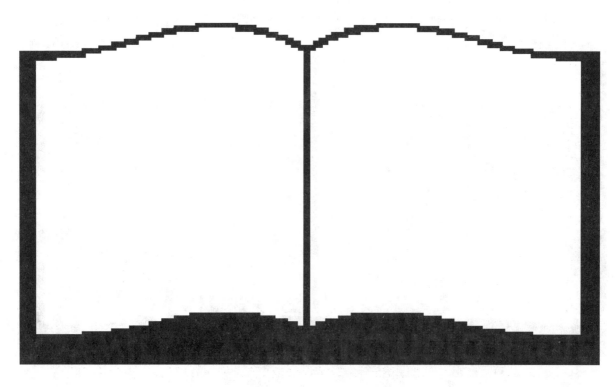

MY FAMILY ... HYPERSTUDIO PROJECT
COMPUTER TEMPLATE

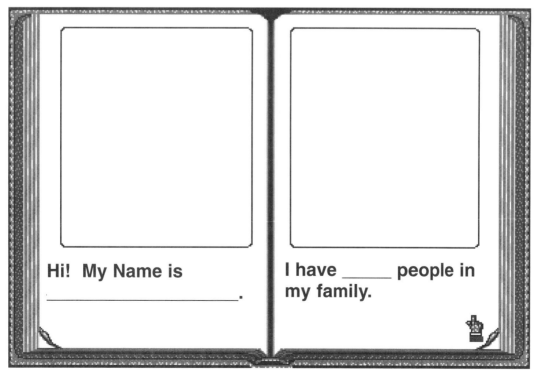

MY FAMILY ... A HYPERSTUDIO PROJECT COMPUTER TEMPLATE, *(cont.)*

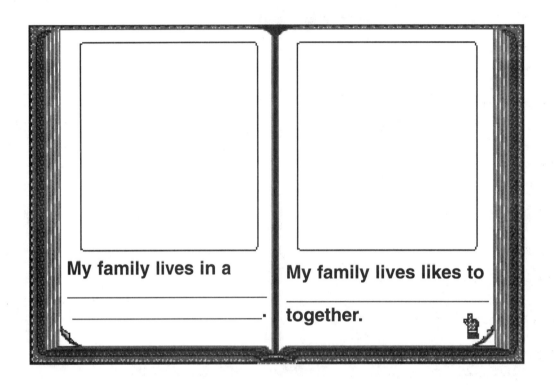

My family lives in a
_____
_____.

My family lives likes to
_____
together.

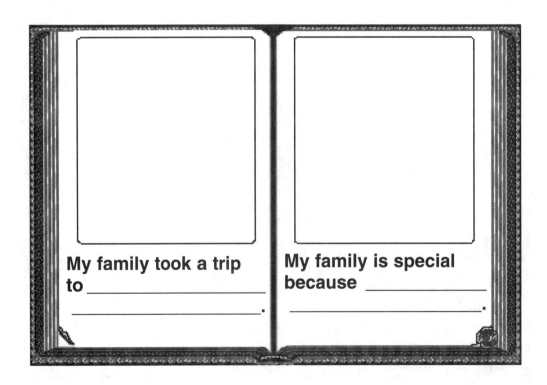

My family took a trip to _____
_____.

My family is special because _____
_____.

CLASS BIRTHDAY BOOK ... A BOOK WRITING ACTIVITY

Who has the same birth month as you? Conduct a birthday survey to find out who has the same birthday month as you and which month has the most birthdays.

Grades: 1–3

Duration: two 30-minute sessions

Instructional Objective: The students will enter data into a teacher-created database and sort the data to find information about their classmates' birthdays. Students will create spreadsheets to graph birthday months.

Materials: teacher-created computer template, pages 59; copies of "My Birthday Page," page 58; computer directions, pages 60 and 61

Computer Software: *ClarisWorks*

Procedure:

Before the Computer:

Lead a discussion about birthdays and the various ways in which birthdays are celebrated. Have the students predict what month has the most classroom birthdays.

On the Computer:

Have the students enter their birthday months into the "Class Birthdays Database" and use the find function to determine the number of birthdays in each month. Then, students can enter this data into a spreadsheet to graph the number of birthdays per month.

After the Computer:

Have students make a classroom birthday book. The book should be divided into twelve sections, one section per month. Each section should include a calendar page with students' and the teacher's birthdays highlighted, a birthday page for each student and the teacher, a copy of the "Our Class Birthdays" bar graph, and a list of famous people born in that month. This book can sent home on each student's birthday to be shared with the student's family.

Internet Links:

Interactive Birthday Calendar—Enter your birthday and receive a list of famous people born on your birth date.
http://www.eb.com/calendar/ca12.htm

Countdown—This site calculates the seconds, minutes, or days until your birthday.
http://www.spiders.com/ogi-bin/countdown

Famous Birthdays—What famous person was born on your birthday?
http://oeonline.com/~edog/bday.html

Extended Activity:

Write about a famous person born in your birthday month.

MY BIRTHDAY PAGE

My name is _____.

I am _____ years old.

My birthday is _____.

A famous person born in my birthday month is _____.

My favorite kind of birthday cake is _____.

If I could have the birthday gift of my dreams, it would be a (an)

_____.

If I could take a trip on my birthday, I would go to _____

_____.

My birthday wish is _____

_____

_____

_____

_____

CLASS BIRTHDAYS COMPUTER TEMPLATE

1. Open the "Our Class Birthdays" database.

2. Search the database to find out how many students had birthdays in each month. For each month, do a "find" search to find out how many boys and girls had a birthday in that month.

3. Write the data in the table below.

Month	Number	Names
January		
February		
March		
April		
May		
June		
July		
August		
September		
October		
November		
December		

CLASS BIRTHDAYS TEMPLATE *(cont.)*

4. Open a new spreadsheet. Enter the data from the table above. (Your spreadsheet should look like the picture below except it will have your data.)

	A	B
1	Month	Number
2	Jan.	3
3	Feb.	5
4	Mar.	6
5	Apr.	3
6	May	2
7	June	3
8	July	4
9	Aug.	1
10	Sept.	4
11	Oct.	2
12	Nov.	1
13	Dec.	0

5. Click and drag to highlight all cells with information.

6. Pull down the Options menu to Make Chart. Click on Bar Graph.

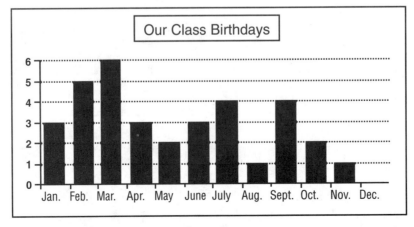

CLASS BIRTHDAY CALENDAR DIRECTIONS

1. Open *ClarisWorks.*

2. Click on the Use Assistant or Stationery box. Then click the OK button.

3. Choose Calendar and click the OK button.

4. At the Calendar Assistant welcome screen, click the Next button.

5. At the Calendar Assistant screen, choose the month and year for the calendar you want to create. Then click the Create button.

6. At the calendar screen, type the names of the students who have birthdays for that month in the date cells. Under the Format menu, change Alignment to Center and Text Size to 12 point.

7. Open the Library under the File menu and choose the birthday cake graphic from Events & Holidays. Click the Use button.

8. Drag the birthday cake graphic to the birthday cell. Under the Arrange menu, choose Transform and scale graphic 25%. Place graphic in the lower left corner. Note: You can duplicate the graphic under the Edit menu and drag the graphics to the other birthday cells.

9. Print a copy of the calendar.

10. You will repeat this process for each month of the year. These pages will be placed in the "Class Birthday Book."

SEPTEMBER

Sunday	Monday	Tuesday	Wednesday	Thursday	Friday	Saturday
	1	2	3	4	5	6
7	8	9	10	11	12	13
14	15	16	17	18	19 Derek	20
21	22	23	24	25	26	27
28	29	30				

CLASS FAVORITES ... A DATABASE/SPREADSHEET ACTIVITY

How well do you know your classmates? Do you know their favorite colors, holidays, or subjects? Enter your favorites into a database and sort the data to find classmates who like the same things that you do.

Grades: 2–3

Duration: three 30-minute sessions

Instructional Objective: The students will enter data into a teacher-created database and sort the data to find information about their classmates' favorite things.

Materials: teacher-created computer template, page 63; copies of "Getting to Know You" and "Things I Know About My Partner" masters on pages 64 and 65; computer directions on pages 66 and 67

Computer Software: *ClarisWorks* or *Microsoft Works*

Procedure:

Before the Computer:

Have the students work in groups of four to brainstorm a list of "class favorites," such as favorite sport, favorite holiday, favorite school subject, etc. Use these lists to create a "Class Favorites" database template like the sample on page 63. Then, have each student complete the "Getting to Know You" activity sheet on page 64 and take it with them to the computer.

On the Computer:

Have the students enter their personal favorites into the "Class Favorites" database and use the "match," "sort," and "find" functions to determine their classmates' favorite things. Each student will analyze this data to find the classmate who has the most similar "favorites."

After the Computer:

Pair each student with a partner who has the most similar "favorites" and have them work together to create Venn diagrams that compare and contrast their favorites. Have them complete the "Things I Know About My Partner" sheet on page 65 to collect information for their Venn diagrams.

Internet Link:

Students can create a "Class Favorites" survey and e-mail it to other classrooms around the world to find out if students have similar favorites.

Extended Activity:

Record the "Class Favorites" data into a spreadsheet and create graphs and charts. These can be put on a bulletin board display or bound together to make a "Class Favorites" book.

OUR CLASS FAVORITES DATABASE

Our Class Favorites

First Name	Laura
Last Name	Clark
Favorite Color	blue
Favorite Subject	reading
Favorite Sport	basketball
Favorite Food	pizza
Favorite Holiday	Christmas
Favorite Game	Monopoly
Favorite Pet	dog
Favorite Book	Matilda

Records:
1

Unsorted

GETTING TO KNOW YOU

Name _____   Date _____

Complete the sentences in each box. Then open the "Our Class Favorites" database. Use the "sort," "find," and "match" functions to find classmates who have the same favorites as you. Write their names in the boxes below.

My favorite color is	My favorite subject is
My favorite sport is	My favorite food is
My favorite holiday is	My favorite game is
My favorite pet is	My favorite book is

Does anyone have all of the same favorites as you do? (That person's name would have to appear in each box.) Write that person's name.

_____

THINGS I KNOW ABOUT MY PARTNER

My name is

_____

My partner's name is

_____

This is a picture of my partner.

Our Favorites

Favorite	Partner's Favorite	My Favorite	Same	Different
Color				
Subject				
Sport				
Food				
Holiday				
Game				
Pet				
Book				

What things were the same?

_____

What things were different?

_____

CLASS FAVORITES SPREADSHEET

1. Choose a "class favorite" to explore, such as favorite pet.

   Write your choice here: _____

2. Open the "Our Class Favorites" database.

3. Search the database to find all of the different choices. For example, favorite pets might include dog, cat, fish, bird, hamster, gerbil, or snake. Write the choices you find in the table below.

4. For each choice, do a "find" search to find out how many people chose that as their favorite. Write the number in the table below.

5. Open a new spreadsheet. Enter the data from the table.

Choice	Number

	A	B
1	Choice	Number
2	dog	9
3	cat	7
4	fish	3
5	bird	2
6	hamster	2
7	gerbil	1
8	snake	1

Favorites Table   Spreadsheet Example

CLASS FAVORITES SPREADSHEET *(cont.)*

6. Select Make Chart from the Options menu. Make a bar graph.

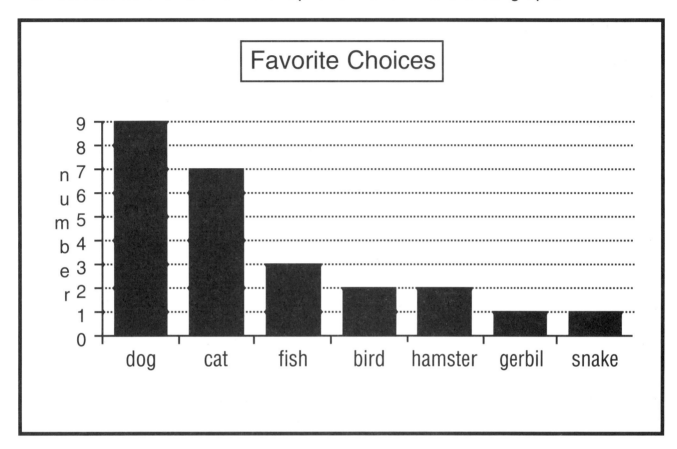

7. Print your bar graph.

8. Analyze the data on your bar graph. Write four sentences to tell what you have learned about the class favorite you just explored.

_____

_____

_____

_____

_____

_____

A POSTAGE STAMP ... A DRAWING ACTIVITY

Some postage stamps honor special events and people. Honor a person who has made a difference in your school life by designing a special postage stamp for him or her.

Grades: 1–3

Duration: 30 minutes

Instructional Objective: The students will use a paint/draw program to design a postage stamp in honor of a special person.

Materials: teacher-created computer template, page 69

Computer Software: *ClarisWorks* or *Microsoft Works*

Procedure:

Before the Computer:

Brainstorm a list of people in the school who help students. Discuss why these people are special and describe the ways that they help students. Explain that some postage stamps are designed to honor people for their accomplishments. Show the students examples of stamps that honor special people. Talk about why these people were honored. Help the students choose a person in the school to honor by designing a special stamp to commemorate his or her life.

On the Computer:

Have the students use the paint/draw application to design a postage stamp that shows why their chosen person is special.

After the Computer:

Have students share their postage stamps with the class.

Internet Link:

Stamp Images
http://www.usps.gov/images/stamps

Extended Activities:

1. Design a postage stamp to honor yourself. Tell how you would want to be remembered on a postage stamp.

2. Design a postage stamp to honor your school.

3. Design a postage stamp to honor your community.

POSTAGE STAMP TEMPLATE

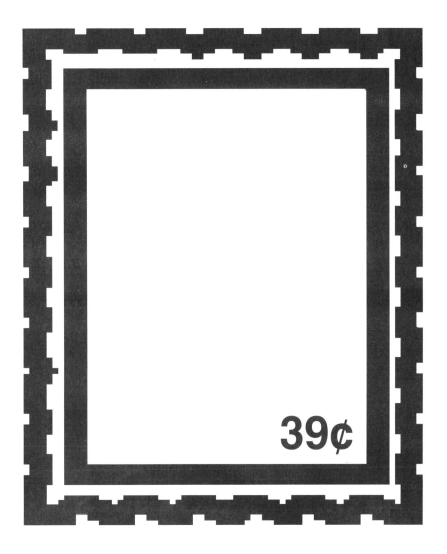

How does the stamp show that the person is special?

_____

_____

Note: Create this template in the drawing or painting application. Name this file Postage Stamp Template and save it as a stationery file. Students can use the paint/draw tools to design the stamp. If you write the question in a text box, students can type their answers on the screen. Each student should print his or her paper and then close the file without saving.

WELCOME TO OUR CLASSROOM BOOK ... A COOPERATIVE GROUP ACTIVITY

Have you ever been a new student in a class or school? How do you think a new student feels? Work in cooperative groups to create "Welcome to Our Classroom" books that will be shared with students new to the classroom.

Grades: 1–3

Duration: three 30-minute sessions

Instructional Objectives: The students will work in groups of four to collect information and write a book that will introduce a new student to the rules, routines, and special aspects of the classroom.

Materials: teacher-created computer template, page 72; copies of planning sheet, page 71

Computer Software: *ClarisWorks* or *Microsoft Works*

Procedure:

Before the Computer:

Discuss the importance of making new students feel welcome in the classroom and ways to do this. Assign students to cooperative groups of four. Have each group brainstorm ten ideas for information a new student would need to know about the classroom. Discuss all of the ideas and pick one for each group to complete. Then have each group complete a rough draft, using the template on page 71.

On the Computer:

Have each group of students use the word processing and paint/draw applications to write and illustrate a page for the "Welcome to Our Classroom" book.

After the Computer:

Have each group of students share their "Welcome to Our Classroom" pages with the class.

Internet Link:

Students can create a "Welcome to Our Classroom" home page.
Look for your community Web site.

Extended Activities:

1. Using the master on page 73, students can write acrostic poems describing themselves for a new student.
2. "Welcome to Our Classroom" books can be written by the previous year's class to be given to the incoming class.
3. "Welcome to Our Community" books can be written to describe the community from a child's view. These books can be printed, and the local chamber of commerce can give them to children moving into the community.

"WELCOME TO OUR CLASSROOM" BOOK PLANNING SHEET

Group Members: _____

Brainstorm items to include in our book to welcome a new student.

1. _____
   _____

2. _____
   _____

3. _____
   _____

4. _____
   _____

5. _____
   _____

6. _____
   _____

7. _____
   _____

8. _____
   _____

9. _____
   _____

10. _____
    _____

"WELCOME TO OUR CLASSROOM" BOOK COMPUTER TEMPLATE

Note: The teacher should create this template on the computer and save it as a stationery file prior to students beginning their work.

Sketch a picture of what each page will look like in the box and write the text below.

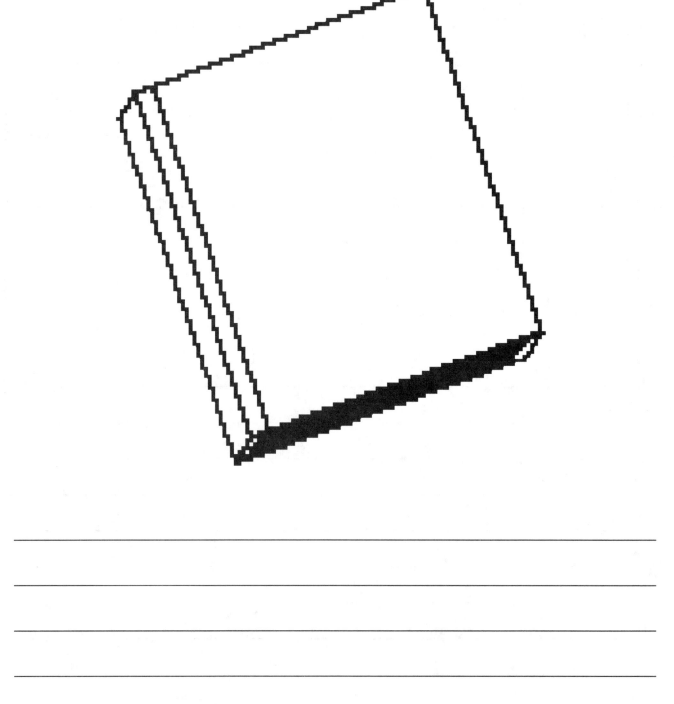

_____

_____

_____

_____

ALL ABOUT ME

Write an acrostic poem that describes you to a new student. Click on the Caps Lock Key. Enter each letter of your name in the column cells. Then enter an adjective that begins with each letter of your name in the adjective column cells. Use a different font for each letter and adjective. Change the font under the Format menu.

	A	B
1	Letter	Adjective
2		
3		
4		
5		
6		
7		
8		
9		
10		

Note: The teacher should create this spreadsheet template on the computer before students begin working. Drag the mouse to highlight all of the cells, click on the Format menu, and choose 24-point.

A PICTURE MAP OF THE CLASSROOM ... A DRAWING ACTIVITY

A map shows where important things are located. A picture map can show where important things are located in the classroom.

Grades: 2–3

Duration: 30 minutes

Instructional Objectives: The students will use a teacher-created map template and the paint/draw application to create a map of the classroom.

Materials: directions for computer work, page 75

Computer Software: *ClarisWorks* or *Microsoft Works*

Procedure:

Before the Computer:

Show examples of maps. Have students brainstorm a list of important items that should be included on a picture map of the classroom. Show and discuss the sample on page 76.

On the Computer:

Have the students use the paint/draw application to create a picture map of the classroom.

After the Computer:

Include the map in the "Welcome to Our Classroom" books made in the previous activity.

Internet Links:

Mapmaker, Mapmaker, Make Me a Map—Explains what a map maker does and tells about different kinds of maps

http://oki.ur.utk.edu.ut2kids/maps

U.S. Gazetteer—See maps and census information for any location in the United States. Just type the name of the community, state, and zip code.

http://www.census.gov/ogi-bin/gazetteer

Extended Activities:

1. Work in cooperative groups to make picture maps of the cafeteria or playground.

2. Make picture maps of students' bedrooms.

A PICTURE MAP OF THE CLASSROOM

1. Draw a large rectangle.

2. Use these symbols to create a picture map of your classroom. Use Duplicate under the Edit menu to copy a symbol. Drag the symbol to the desired place on the classroom map. Use Transform under the Arrange menu to rotate objects 90°.

3. Use the arrow tool to select the sample map and click the Delete key to clear.

4. Create your map and print a copy.

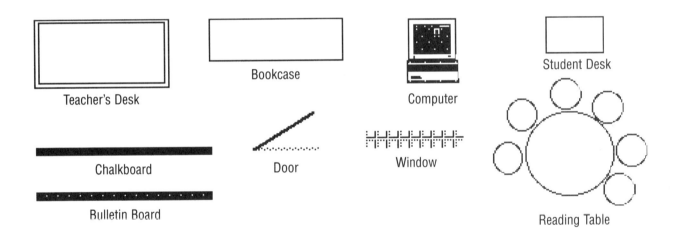

Teacher's Desk

Bookcase

Computer

Student Desk

Chalkboard

Door

Window

Bulletin Board

Reading Table

SAMPLE CLASSROOM MAP

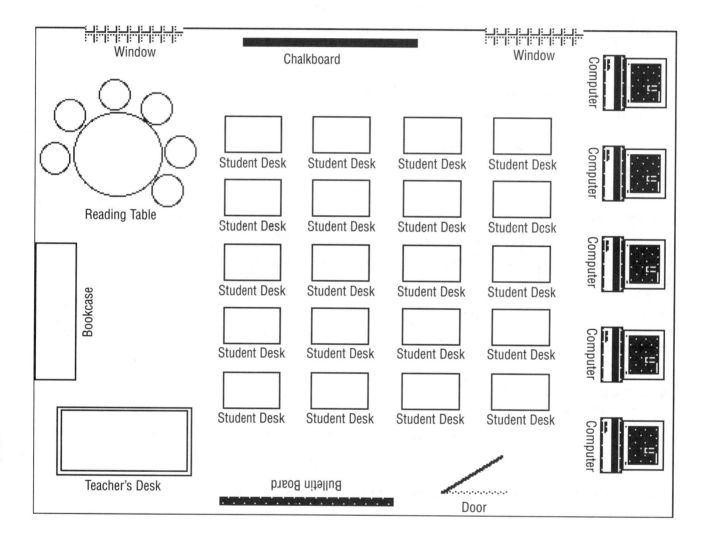

A BIOGLYPH ... A DRAWING ACTIVITY

Hieroglyphics was a system of picture writing used in ancient Egypt. It can be lots of fun to use pictures to deliver a message or tell a story. Use a form of hieroglyphics called "Bioglyphics" to tell something about yourself.

Grades: 1-3

Duration: 30 minutes

Instructional Objective: The students will use the paint/draw application to create a "bioglyph," a picture that tells something about themselves.

Materials: copy of Bioglyph Key and Sample, page 79

Computer Software: *ClarisWorks* or *Microsoft Works*

Procedure:

Before the Computer:

Discuss with the students that hieroglyphics was a system of picture writing used in ancient Egypt, and that this system consisted of 21 one-letter signs. Show them a copy of Egyptian hieroglyphics and the English alphabet equivalent. This chart can be found at *http://www.idsc.gov.eg/tourism/tor trn.htm* or it can be enlarged from page 80. Then, show students the key and sample on page 79.

On the Computer:

Have the students create "bioglyphs" to tell about themselves.

After the Computer:

Have the students share their "bioglyphs."

Internet Links:

Enter text to be translated into hieroglyphics. See the sample on page 80.

http://www.idsc.gov.eg/tourism/tor_trn.htm

Write your name as it would have been written in hieroglyphics. See page 78.

http://khety.iut.univ-paris8.fr/~rosmond/nomhiero.html

History of hieroglyphics

http://khety.iut.univ-paris8.fr/~rosmond/Intro/Intro.html
http://daec.obspm.fr/~wacren/

Extended Activities:

1. Write your first and last names in hieroglyphics, using copies of page 78.
2. Create a new hieroglyphic alphabet.
3. Cut pictures from magazines and catalogs to create a visual alphabet.
4. Write an alphabet big book.

WRITE YOUR NAME IN EGYPTIAN HIEROGLYPHS

Open *http://khety.iut.univ-paris8.fr/~rosmond/nomhiero.html.* Enter your name.
Then press the send button. Your name will appear in hieroglyphs.

Nom en hieroglyphes

Entrez phonétiquement votre nom, en n'utilisant que les caractères entre 'a' et 'z'. **Attention !** le mécanisme de cache de certains butineurs peut vous jouer des tours si vous tapez plusieurs noms : utilisez dans ce cas la fonction reload.

Write you name phonetically. **Please !** note that some browsers cache the result, and may send you an outdated file for the second name you ask. If you always get the first name you typed, simply ask the browser to reload the page.

Fran Clark

[Envoyer / Send]   [Effacer / Erase]

Votre nom en Hieroglyphes/Your Name in Hieroglyphs

Make up new symbols that represent you. For example, if you like to play soccer, use a picture of a soccer ball to represent one of the letters in your name. Write your name below, using symbols that represent you!

BIOGLYPH KEY AND SAMPLE

◯	girl	⌢	goes to daycare
◯	boy	ε	has a brother
⊙	blue eyes	₹	has a sister
⬮	brown eyes	●	# of brothers and sisters
◉	green eyes	∨	has a pet
₹	dark hair	◯	has a dog
❘	light hair	△	has a cat
>	rides car to school	▢	has a bird
∠	rides bus to school	⬭	has a fish
∨	walks to school	⊢⊣	new to this school
↝	wears glasses	⌣	not new to this school

This person is an eight-year-old girl. She has brown hair and blue eyes. She did not go to this school last year. Her mom drives her to school. She has two brothers and a sister. She also has two dogs and a cat.

EGYPTIAN HIEROGLYPHS AND ENGLISH ALPHABET EQUIVALENT

This chart was taken from *http://www.idsc.gov.eg/tourism/tor_trn.htm*

• A	• B	• C	• D	• F
• G	• H	• I	• J	• K
• L	• M	• N	• O	• P
• Q	• R	• S	• T	• U
• V	• W	• X	• Y	• Z

My name is _____.

My name written in hieroglyphics is

_____

_____

_____

WHERE DO WE COME FROM? ... A SPREADSHEET ACTIVITY

Where do you come from? Were you born in the country you live in now? Were your parents or grandparents born in the country you live in now? Research your cultural ancestry to find out.

Grades: 2–3

Duration: two 30-minute sessions

Instructional Objective: The students will research their cultural ancestries and make bar graphs to illustrate the cultural diversity of the class.

Materials: directions for computer work, page 82; copies of "Flags," page 83

large world map; paper flags; color printer; Internet connection

Computer Software: *ClarisWorks* or *Microsoft Works, Netscape Navigator* or *Internet Explorer*

Procedure:

Before the Computer:

Note: This part of the lesson will most likely need to be continued to the following day so that students can discuss family origins at home.

Discuss that our family ancestors came to America from other countries. List all the different cultures that make up the class ancestry. Locate these countries on a world map.

On the Computer:

Have the students use the Internet to find illustrations of the flags of the countries of the world. Students can draw the flag(s) that represent(s) their cultural heritage, using the master on page 83. Then, have the students enter the collected data and create spreadsheets, using the directions on page 82.

After the Computer:

Attach the flags to the world map. Print bar graphs to add to the display.

Internet Links:

Flags of the Nations of the World—250 images plus flag facts and trivia
http://www.globalserve.net/~photodsk/flags/flags.html

World Flags—pictures of flags from around the world
http://www.adfa.oz.au/cs/flg

Extended Activity:

Create surveys and bar graphs to illustrate the cultural diversity of the school.

WHERE DO WE COME FROM? SPREADSHEET DIRECTIONS

1. Countries have their own flags but so do cultural groups, such as Native Americans. List in the table below all of the cultural areas that have flags. Count the number of flags for each area and record that number in the table below.

Cultural Area	Number

2. Open the spreadsheet application and enter your data.

3. Drag the mouse to highlight all cells in the spreadsheet.

4. Under the Options menu, choose Make a Chart. Click on the Bar and Horizontal buttons.

5. Double-click inside the graph. Click the Axes button. Type Number of Students for the Y Axis and type Cultural Area for the X Axis.

6. Click the Labels button. Type Where Do We Come From? in the Title box and click the Legend box to deselect legend.

7. Print a copy of the bar graph.

A Sample Bar Graph

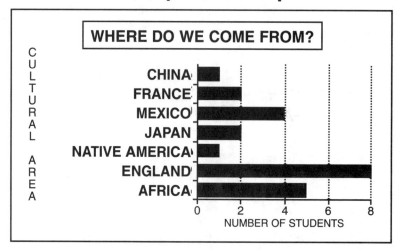

FLAGS

1. Access the Internet. Enter the following URL: *http://www.adfa.oz.au/cs/flg* and open the World Flags Web site.

2. Find the flags that represent your cultural heritage. Sketch them in the boxes below.

3. Use crayons or markers to color your flags.

4. Cut out the boxes and place them on the correct countries on the world map.

Name:_____

Country or Culture: _____

Name:_____

Country or Culture: _____

MULTICULTURAL COOKBOOK ... A WRITING ACTIVITY

Many of the foods Americans eat have come from different immigrant groups. For example, spaghetti was brought to America by the Italians.

Grades: 2–3

Duration: 30 minutes

Instructional Objective: The students will share traditional recipes from their cultural heritages.

Materials: teacher-created computer template, page 85; family recipe; cookbooks

Computer Software: *ClarisWorks* or *Microsoft Works*

Procedure:

Before the Computer:

Discuss foods we eat that have come from various immigrant groups. Brainstorm a list of foods and identify the countries they come from. Have a variety of cookbooks available for resources.

On the Computer:

Have each student enter on the template a favorite traditional recipe from his or her cultural heritage.

After the Computer:

Print the recipes and bind them into a "Multicultural Cookbook." Make copies for each child to take home.

Internet Links:

Culture Quest—Take a tour of cultures around the world.
http://www.ipl.org/youth/cquest/index.html

World Safari—Learn about the food, customs, and history of people in other countries.
http://www.supersurf.com/

Extended Activity:

Have the students prepare their recipes at home (under adult supervision) and bring them to share with the class. Or, choose a few to make and sample in class.

MULTICULTURAL COOKBOOK TEMPLATE

Your Name:_____

Name of Dish:_____

Country: _____

Ingredients:_____

_____

_____

Directions:_____

_____

_____

_____.

WHAT IS A ...? POEM ... A SLIDE SHOW ACTIVITY

Many of the words that we use come from other countries. Two examples are lariat (Spanish, la riata) and beef (French, baenf).

Grades: 2–3

Duration: three 30-minute sessions

Instructional Objective: The students will write a poem based on a foreign word.

Materials: copies of planning sheet, page 87; directions for computer work, pages 88 and 89

Computer Software: *ClarisWorks*

Procedure:

Before the Computer:

Explain that many of the words we use every day come from various culture groups. Brainstorm a list of words we use and the countries they originated from. Have students choose words from their own cultural heritages to create a poem.

On the Computer:

Have students use the Internet to find words from their cultural heritages. Then, have them write their poems and sketch their illustrations on the "What Is a...?" Planning Sheet on page 87. Finally, have the students enter their poems into the slide show application and add illustrations.

After the Computer:

Have the students share their slide shows.

Internet Links:

Foreign Language for Travelers—Translate words and phrases into 50 different languages.
http://www.travlang.com/languages

Foreign Language Resources on the Web—a starting point to mine the Web for foreign language and culture specific resources
http://www.itp.berkeley.edu/~thorne/HumanResources.html

Extended Activity:

Compile a "What Is a ...?" big book with the completed poems.

WHAT IS A ...? POEM SLIDE SHOW PLANNING SHEET

Writing the Poem

1. Choose a word from another language that names a person, place, or thing.

2. Use this format to write the poem:

    - Line 1 of the poem asks the question, "What Is a (an) _____?
    - Line 2 reads: "A(An) _____ is...
    - Lines 3–7 answer the question.
    - Line 8 tells the language for the word chosen.

3. Here is a sample poem:

    > Perro
    >
    > What is a perro?
    >
    > A perro is...
    >
    > a man's best friend,
    >
    > eyes to a blind person,
    >
    > an enemy to an intruder,
    >
    > a home to a flea.
    >
    > Perro is Spanish for dog.

WHAT IS A ...? POEM SLIDE SHOW DIRECTIONS

Setting up the Slide Show Application

1. Open a Drawing document.

2. Go to Format menu and choose Document. Change the margins to one inch and Pages Across to 9.

3. Go to File menu and choose Page Setup. Change paper orientation to Landscape.

4. Go to Options menu and choose Hide Graphics Grid.

5. Go to View menu and choose Page View.

6. Each line of the poem will be a slide in the slide show.

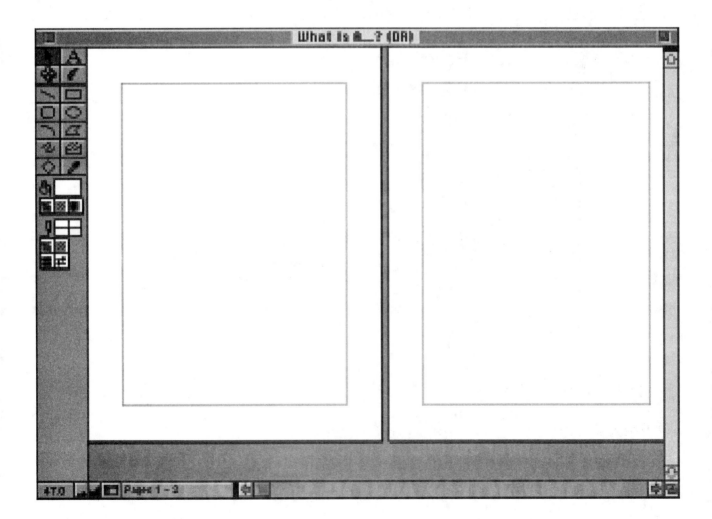

WHAT IS A ...? POEM SLIDE SHOW DIRECTIONS

Viewing the Slide Show

Running a Slide Show

- Choose Slide Show from the View menu.
- Set viewing options for the slide show.
- Click Start to begin the show.

Viewing Options

- Fit to screen - resizes the slide to fit the screen.
- Center - shows the slide in the middle of the screen.
- Show cursor - makes the arrow pointer visible during the slide show.
- Fade - makes one slide dissolve into darkness and the next slide illuminate gradually.
- Loop - makes the slide show run continuously.
- Advance every - paces the slide show.

```
┌─Slide Options ──────────────────────────┐
│  ☒ Fit to screen      ☐ Fade           │
│  ☒ Center             ☐ Loop           │
│  ☒ Show cursor        ☐ Advance every  │
│                        ▣ 5  seconds     │
│     ☐ Background                         │
│     ▣ Border                             │
└──────────────────────────────────────────┘
```

Stopping a Slide Show

- Press the "q" key.
- From the slide show dialog box, click Done or Cancel.

MULTICULTURAL CALENDAR ... AN INTERNET RESEARCH ACTIVITY

Many of the holidays that we celebrate originated in different cultures. Research the traditions of different cultures through the creation of a multicultural calendar.

Grades: 2–3

Duration: three 30-minute sessions

Instructional Objective: The students will research the traditions of different cultures and create a multicultural calendar.

Materials: copies of page 91; Internet access; CD-ROM encyclopedias

Computer Software: *ClarisWorks, Microsoft Works,* CD-ROM encyclopedias

Procedure:

Before the Computer:

Discuss the holiday traditions that students celebrate and the country in which they originated. Brainstorm a list of cultures students would like to know more about. Divide the class into groups of two or three and assign a culture to each group.

On the Computer:

During session one, have groups use the Internet and CD-ROM encyclopedias to find important calendar dates in the traditions of their assigned cultures.

During session two, assign each group a month. Using the calendar on page 91, have the students fill in the dates for holidays and other important dates for their assigned culture for that month. Students can decorate the calendar month with patterns and symbols from their assigned cultures.

After the Computer:

Have the students choose one holiday or important date from their month to illustrate. Students mount their calendars and illustrations on pieces of 11" x 17" colored poster board. The poster boards can be bound together to make a classroom multicultural calendar.

Internet Links:

Multicultural Calendar—Search by month, day, or year to find out about holidays around the world.
http://www.kidlink.org/KIDPROG/MCC

The World Book of Traditions—Students can submit the ways they celebrate special days and view what others have submitted about special days.
http://mgfx.com/holidays

Extended Activity:

Have students create a " How We Celebrate Special Days" book.

CALENDAR

Sunday	Monday	Tuesday	Wednesday	Thursday	Friday	Saturday

PEANUTS AND PEOPLE ...
A MULTIDIMENSIONAL ACTIVITY

At first glance, two peanuts might seem exactly alike. But when you look closely, you might discover some differences. Did you know that people are like peanuts?

Grades: 1–3

Duration: three 30-minute sessions

Instructional Objective: The students will discover how people are the same in some ways and different in others.

Materials: copies of data collection and fact sheets, pages 93 and 94; "Peanut is Missing" Sign directions, page 95; one peanut per student; balance with metric weights; metric ruler; magnifying glass

Computer Software: *ClarisWorks, Microsoft Works*

Procedure:

Before the Computer:
During session one, the teacher should put the students into groups of four. Then, give each student a peanut to observe. Instruct each group to discuss how the peanuts are alike and how they are different.
During session two, the teacher should give each student a peanut and ask the students to observe and record facts about their peanuts on the data collection and facts sheets. Students can use the following: centimeter ruler to record the length and width of the peanut, balance to measure its weight, and a magnifying glass to note its distinguishing characteristics.
During session three, the students' peanuts should be laid on a table so they can identify their peanuts using the information recorded on their data collection and fact sheets. Help the students compare and contrast their peanuts by noting similarities and differences.

On the Computer:
During session one, have students use the word processor to make lists of peanut characteristics.
During session two, have them use the spreadsheet application to create a bar graph that compares and contrasts the groups' peanuts' weights, lengths, and widths.
During session three, have the students use the paint/draw application, the information recorded on the data collection and fact sheets, and the directions on page 95 to create a "Peanut Is Missing" Sign.

After the Computer:
Discuss how peanuts, like people, each have characteristics that are similar and different.

Internet Links:
Multicultural Calendar—Search by month, day, or year to find out about holidays around the world.
http://www.kidlink.org/KIDPROG/MCC
The World Book of Traditions—Students can submit the ways that they celebrate special days and view what others have submitted about special days.
http://mgfx.com/holidays

Extended Activities:
Compare peanuts without shells to peanuts with shells on a Venn diagram. Or, let students choose to compare themselves with a friend. A Venn diagram master is provided on page 96.

PEANUT DATA COLLECTION SHEET

Directions: Choose one peanut from the bowl. Observe your peanut. Use the measurement devices to help you record some information about your peanut. You will use this information to write some facts about your peanut. These facts will help you find your peanut later. Keep accurate records!

My peanut is _____ (color).

My peanut's shape is _____ (round, oval, or oblong?).

My peanut is _____ cm long and _____ cm wide.

My peanut weighs _____ g.

My peanut looks like this:

Which group member's peanut weighs the most? _____

Which group member's peanut is the longest? _____

Which group member's peanut has the same shape as yours? _____

PEANUT FACT SHEET

How is your peanut the same as the other group members' peanuts? _____

_____

How is your peanut different from the other group members' peanuts? _____

_____

Some Facts About My Peanut

My peanut is _____

My peanut is _____

My peanut is _____

My peanut is _____

Write a short descriptive paragraph about your peanut.

_____

_____

_____

_____

PEANUT IS MISSING SIGN

Directions: Your peanut is missing. You want to find it. Create a "Missing Peanut" sign. First, draw a picture of your peanut on the sign below. Then write some sentences to describe your peanut. Be sure to write about your peanut's special characteristics!

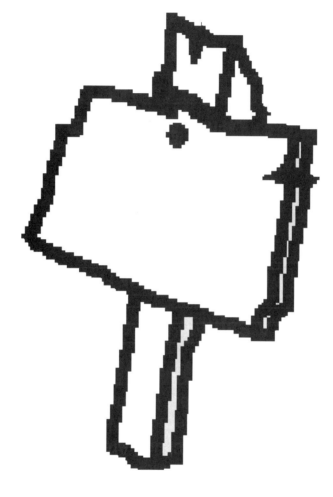

_____

_____

_____

_____

WE ARE ALIKE ... WE ARE DIFFERENT

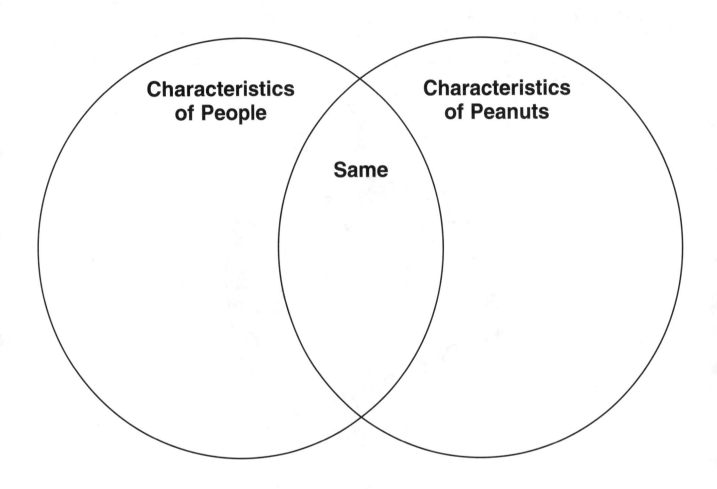

**Characteristics
of People**

Same

**Characteristics
of Peanuts**

Write some sentences that tell how your objects are alike.

_____

_____

_____

_____

_____

FOREIGN LANGUAGE NUMBER BOOK ... A BOOK WRITING ACTIVITY

Uno, dos, tres ... can you continue counting in Spanish? If you need some help, you can go to The Foreign Language for Travelers Web site. You will find helpful words and phrases in fifty foreign languages!

Grades: 1–3

Duration: two 30-minute sessions

Instructional Objective: The purpose of this lesson is to introduce the numbers one through ten in a foreign language.

Materials: teacher-created computer template (See the example on page 99); copies of planning sheet, page 98

Computer Software: *ClarisWorks, Microsoft Works*

Procedure:

Before the Computer:

The teacher should open the Foreign Language for Travelers Web site at the address listed below and click on the Spanish flag to choose Spanish. Then choose "numbers" and click on each number word to hear the Spanish pronunciation. Have the students repeat and count to ten. Allow them to choose a language from their cultural heritage and repeat this procedure. For the numbers one through ten, have students write each number, the English word, and the foreign equivalent on the Foreign Language Number Book Planning Sheet.

On the Computer:

Have the students open the Foreign Language for Travelers Web site, find the language of their cultural heritage, and work with the numbers one through ten. Have them enter the number, the English number word, and the foreign language number word for the numbers 1–10 on a teacher-created computer template. They can use clip art to illustrate their number pages.

After the Computer:

Have the students share their various languages. Students can then share their number books with younger students or take them home to share with younger siblings.

Internet Link:

Foreign Language for Travelers—Translate words and phrases into 50 languages.
http://www.travlang.com/languages

Extended Activity:

Students can create foreign language picture dictionaries.

FOREIGN LANGUAGE NUMBER BOOK PLANNING SHEET

Name _____

Number	English Number Word	Foreign Number Word	Graphic Idea

FOREIGN LANGUAGE NUMBER BOOK COMPUTER TEMPLATE EXAMPLE

***uno* ice-cream cone**

I had **uno** ice-cream cone for dessert.

A TOWN POSTCARD... A WRITING ACTIVITY

Postcards can tell a lot about a place with just a picture and a few words. What special place in your community would you like to share with others?

Grades: 1–3

Duration: 30 minutes

Instructional Objective: The students will use a word processing and paint/draw program to create a town postcard that tells about a special place in the community.

Materials: teacher-created computer template, page 101

Computer Software: *ClarisWorks* or *Microsoft Works*

Procedure:

Before the Computer:

Show the students postcards from local areas of interest. Explain that a postcard can describe a special area of interest with a picture and a few words. Brainstorm a list of postcard-worthy places in the community. Ask them what pictures could be used to describe those areas. Ask students how they would describe a special place in just a few sentences. Allow each student time to create a postcard for a special place of interest in the community.

On the Computer:

Have the students create a town postcard using the teacher-created Town Postcard Template on page 101.

After the Computer:

Have the students send their completed postcards to a pen-pal class.

Internet Link:

Send a Web postcard with your favorite cartoon character.
http://www.wbWebcards.com/ns1_indx.html

Extended Activities:

1. Have a postcard exchange with other classes throughout the United States.

2. Create a postcard for the school.

3. Send postcards to residents in a local nursing home.

A TOWN POSTCARD TEMPLATE

Front of Postcard

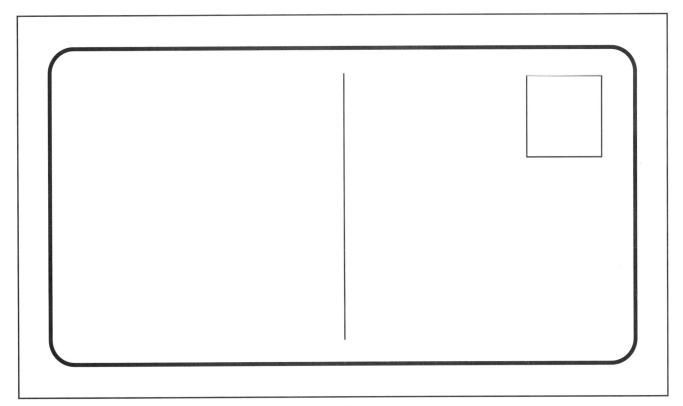

Back of Postcard

OUR TOWN ABC BOOK ... A WRITING ACTIVITY

If you were moving into a new community, what would you like to know about the community?

Grades: 1–3

Duration: 1 hour

Instructional Objective: The students will create an "Our Town ABC Book" about what makes their community special.

Materials: teacher-created computer template, page 103; legal-sized paper

Computer Software: *ClarisWorks* or *Microsoft Works*

Procedure:

Before the Computer:

Allow students time to look at a variety of ABC books to become familiar with the format. Brainstorm a list of things that make the school community special. Assign each student a letter of the alphabet to write about and illustrate with a drawing of something that starts with the assigned letter.

On the Computer:

Have each student create a page for the "Our Town ABC Book" using the teacher-created Our Town ABC Book Template.

After the Computer:

Bind the pages together in a book called "Our Town ABC Book." This book can be shared in the school library or read to younger students.

Internet Links:

Create an "Our Town ABC Book" Web site.

Extended Activities:

1. Exchange "Our Town ABC Books" with classes in other parts of the country.

2. Share copies of the "Our Town ABC Book" with community leaders.

3. Read the "Our Town ABC Book" to residents in a local nursing home.

OUR TOWN ABC BOOK TEMPLATE

A is for

ASSEMBLY LINE ... AN ART ACTIVITY

An assembly line is an arrangement of workers, machines, and equipment in which the product being put together passes consecutively from one station to the next station until the product is assembled.

Grades: 2–3

Duration: 30 minutes

Instructional Objective: The students will assemble a digitized clown, using the drawing application.

Materials: copies of Digitized Clown Face Sample, page 105

Computer Software: *ClarisWorks* or *Microsoft Works*

Procedure:

Before the Computer:

Define the term assembly line and identify products that are made on an assembly line. Explain that in the assembly line each worker does a different job and that each job is an important link in the process. Divide the students into groups of five.

On the Computer:

Give each group of students a completed "Digitized Clown" picture to serve as a model. Use different-colored ink or textures for each part of the clown's face. Have each student create an assigned part of the clown's face. Students takes turns at the computer until the clown face is completed. Students should make a copy of the completed picture for each group member.

After the Computer:

Check each picture against the model. Share the assembly-line pictures.

Internet Link:

Cars and Stuff—take a tour of an automobile factory to see how cars are built.
http://www.ipl.org/youth/cars/

Extended Activities:

1. Make a list of products that are made on an assembly line.

2. Create a flow chart to describe the "Digitized Clown Face" picture process.

DIGITIZED CLOWN FACE SAMPLE

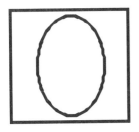 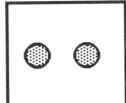   

OUR TOWN MAP ... A MAPPING ACTIVITY

You have been asked to design a community. What kind of places do communities need?

Grades: 2–3

Duration: 1 hour

Instructional Objective: The student groups will create an imaginary town map.

Materials: Town Map Sample on page 107, clipart, poster board, black construction-paper strips

Computer Software: *ClarisWorks* or *Microsoft Works*

Procedure:

Before the Computer:

Discuss what kinds of places communities need and brainstorm a class list. Put students into groups of four. Give each group a large piece of poster board and black construction-paper strips. Have the students glue strips of black construction paper on the poster board to make a basic town grid with a series of intersecting streets to create blocks and open spaces. Use the sample on page 107 to show students. Have them name the streets once their grids are complete.

On the Computer:

Have students use clip art and the paint/draw application to design symbols to represent various locations within the community, such as schools, hospitals, churches, and stores. Tell students that they will need to design a large symbol to be placed on the map and an identical smaller symbol to become part of the map key. Show students how to scale the pictures to make the smaller pictures larger.

After the Computer:

Have the students use colored markers to color the symbols and place them on their imaginary town maps.

Internet Links:

Find the Web site for your community or a community in your area.

Extended Activity:

Let students use these maps to practice map skills. Have them pick a mystery spot on their maps and give clues to help students find the location on their maps.

TOWN MAP SAMPLE

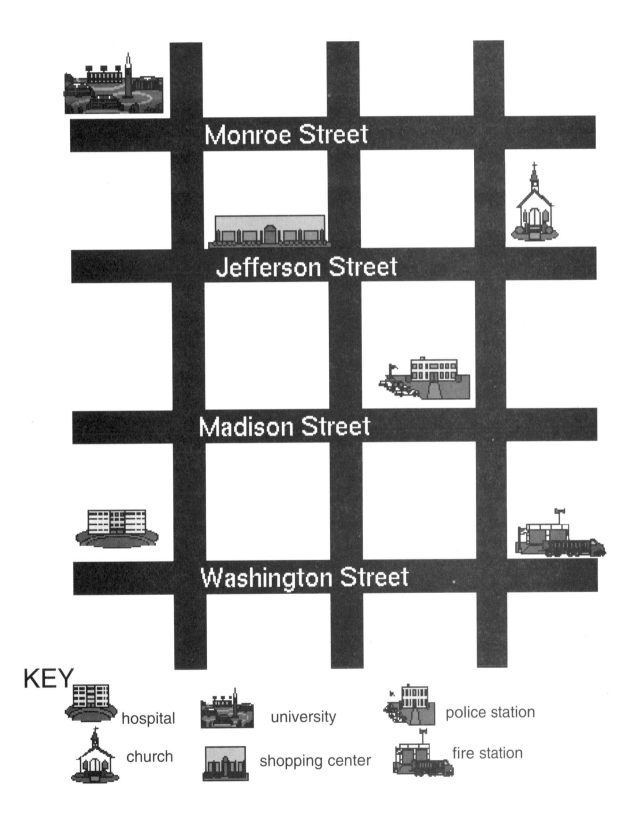

PIZZA, COMPUTERS, AND KIDS ... A CROSS-CURRICULAR UNIT

Let's learn how a business operates by forming an imaginary pizza company! This makes a great end-of-the-year parent event to exhibit computer-generated work and to showcase computer skills that students have acquired.

Grades: 2–3

Duration: one to two weeks

Technology Objectives:

The students will

- conduct a survey
- create a spreadsheet
- enter data into a spreadsheet
- create charts and graphs using data from a spreadsheet
- read and interpret different kinds of charts and graphs
- enter a formula into a spreadsheet to determine the cost of a specific number of pizzas
- analyze spreadsheet data to determine the best value for a specific number of pizzas
- research the nutritional value of different brands of pizza
- create a database
- use the database "sort" and "find" functions to analyze nutritional information to help determine the most healthful pizza
- use the paint/draw application to design a logo for an imaginary pizza company
- use the paint/draw application to design an advertising flyer for the company
- use the word processing application to write a commercial for the company
- use the word processing application to write an original pizza recipe for the company
- use CD-ROM encyclopedias or Internet resources to research the origin of pizza
- use *HyperStudio* to create a TV commercial for the pizza company.

PIZZA, COMPUTERS, AND KIDS ... A CROSS-CURRICULAR UNIT *(cont.)*

Cross-Curricular Objectives:

The students will

- write creatively about selected topics
- compose simple, original paragraphs
- write a business letter
- proofread and revise writing
- compare and contrast items
- construct charts and graphs
- interpret charts and graphs
- solve problems, using charts and graphs
- use reference materials
- know the definitions of nutrients and nutrition
- add and subtract money
- add multidigit numbers
- subtract up to two 3-digit numbers
- identify fractions
- compare two fractions
- create and interpret a flow chart.

Computer Software: *ClarisWorks* or *Microsoft Works, HyperStudio, Netscape Navigator* or *Internet Explorer,* any CD-ROM encyclopedia

Materials: teacher-created computer templates from pages 113–119, 123,124, and 127; students copies of pages 111, 112, 126, and 128; digital camera, scanner; video camera

Procedure:

Before the Computer:

Divide the students into groups of five or six. Tell them that each group will form an imaginary pizza company with the following departments:

- Marketing
- Graphic Design
- Advertising
- Accounting
- Sales
- Research and Development

Each student will be a group leader for a department and, with the teacher's help, will assign tasks to other group members. (If possible, let the students choose departments.)

PIZZA, COMPUTERS, AND KIDS ... A CROSS-CURRICULAR UNIT *(cont.)*

On the Computer: Computer activities are incorporated within the six departments of the imaginary pizza company as follows:

Marketing: Each group will survey a grade level to determine students' favorite kinds of pizza. The students can create a survey form (or use the sample on page 111) and conduct surveys in individual classrooms. Then, have them enter the data by grade level into a spreadsheet and use the data to create graphs and charts (like the samples on page 112) to illustrate each grade level's pizza preferences. This activity can be extended to include the whole school's favorite pizza.

Graphic Design: Have the students use the paint/draw application to design a company logo and a storefront for an imaginary pizza company. Master activity sheets are on pages 113 and 114. Students can make a rough draft on paper first and then work on a teacher-created computer template. They can also design a store menu using the sample on page 115.

Advertising: Have the students use *HyperStudio* to produce a TV commercial that advertises their imaginary pizza company. Activity sheets are on pages 116–118.

Accounting: Have the students obtain information about pizzas from local pizza restaurants and enter the information into a spreadsheet. Students can use this data to compare and contrast the sizes and costs of pizzas to help determine the best pizza values. See the samples on pages 119-121.

Sales: Using a teacher-created template from pages 122–124, have the students write an original recipe and for a new kind of sweet pizza made especially for kids. This will be their imaginary pizza company's product. They can also design an advertising flyer like the sample on page 125.

Research and Development: Have the students review all the pizza recipes and complete the questions on page 126. Students should use pages 127 and 128 to create a database to analyze the nutritional value of selected brands of pizza.

After the Computer:

Invite parents to a class-planned pizza party. Display the students' work and have them tell about their imaginary pizza companies.

Internet Links:

Students can create pizzas using choices of toppings, "order" their creations from the Internet, and see digitalized versions of their pizzas.
http://www2.east.csuchio.edu/~pizza/
Pizza games, history, nutrition information, pizza calculator, favorite topping survey, pizza around the world, and more!
http://www.pizzasite.com/
Pizza facts and history
http://www.eat.com/pizza-lessons/history.html

Extended Activity:

After completing the research on page 128, students can determine whether there are more square inches in a round, square, or rectangular-shaped pizza.

PIZZA PREFERENCE SURVEY DATA COLLECTION SHEET

What Is Your Favorite Kind of Pizza?

Kind of Pizza	Boys	Girls	Adults	Total	Tally
Pepperoni					
Sausage					
Veggie					
Extra Cheese					

1. What kind of pizza do boys like best?

   _____

2. What kind of pizza do girls like best?

   _____

3. What kind of pizza do adults like best?

   _____

4. What kind of pizza do boys like least?

   _____

5. What kind of pizza do girls like least?

   _____

6. What kind of pizza do adults like least?

   _____

7. What kind of pizza do you predict will be the favorite pizza for your grade level?

   _____

8. What kind of pizza do you predict will be the favorite pizza for your school?

   _____

PIZZA PREFERENCE SURVEY DATA COLLECTION SHEET

Sample Pizza Preference Charts and Graphs

Bar Graph

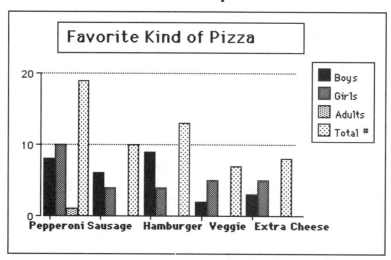

Pie Chart

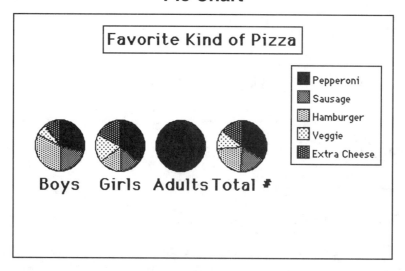

Note: Get on the Internet and visit the Pizza Site at *http://www.pizzasite.com/frames.htm* . You will see a list of favorite pizza toppings. Let students vote for their favorite pizza toppings and then see how their votes compare to others'. Pizza toppings are sorted by popularity. Compare the results at this site to the surveys that were conducted in individual classrooms and school wide.

AN IMAGINARY PIZZA COMPANY LOGO
... A PAINT/DRAW ACTIVITY

A logo is like a symbol. A business logo can tell a lot about a business. What will your company's logo say about its pizza?

Name of Pizza Company: _____

What symbols could be used in your logo design? _____

Sketch your logo here.

```



```

Use the paint/draw tools and clip art to design your imaginary pizza company's logo. Save your company logo to your disk. You will use this logo during this project.

IMAGINARY PIZZA COMPANY STOREFRONT

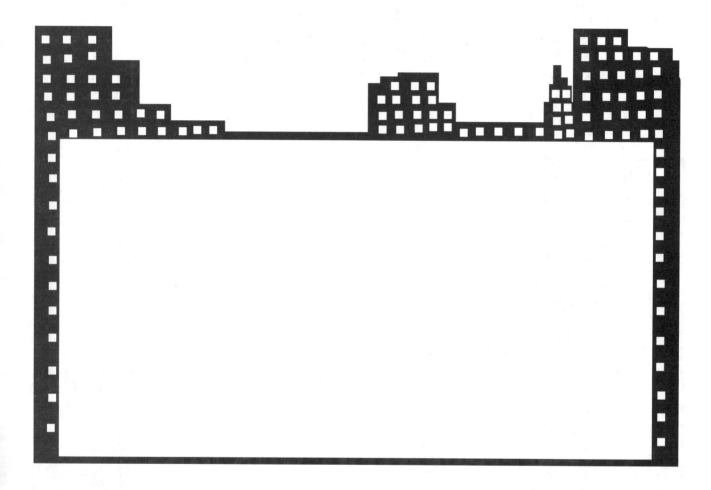

Imagine that your imaginary pizza company is located in a city. What would it look like from a city street? Make a sketch and color it. You need to also include your pizza company name and logo somewhere on the building!

IMAGINARY PIZZA COMPANY MENU

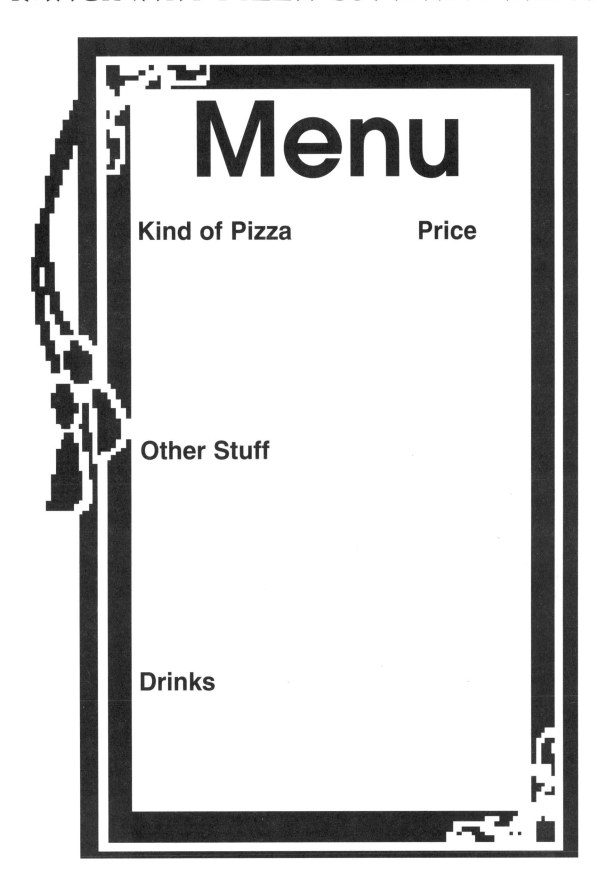

Menu

Kind of Pizza   **Price**

Other Stuff

Drinks

AN IMAGINARY PIZZA COMPANY TV COMMERCIAL ... HYPERSTUDIO STORYBOARD

Sketch scenes for your pizza commercial in the film clip boxes and write the text below.

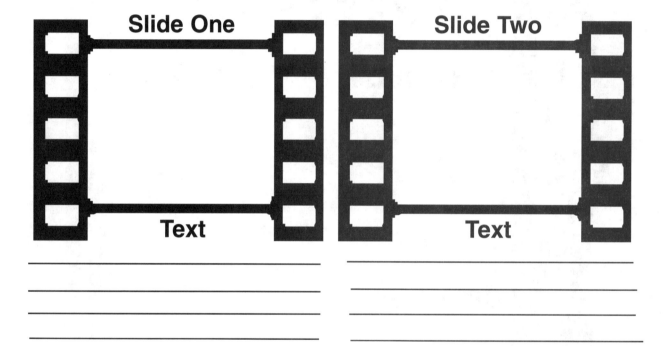

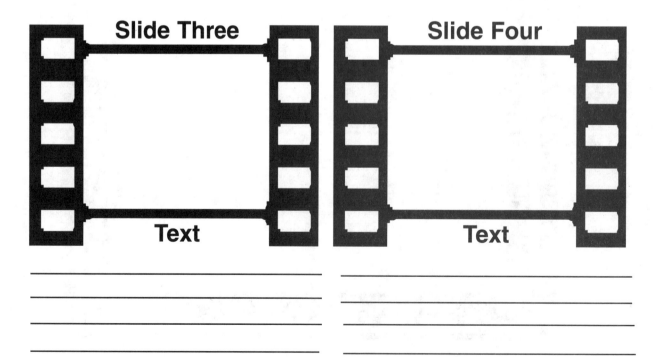

AN IMAGINARY PIZZA COMPANY TV COMMERCIAL ... HYPERSTUDIO STORYBOARD *(cont.)*

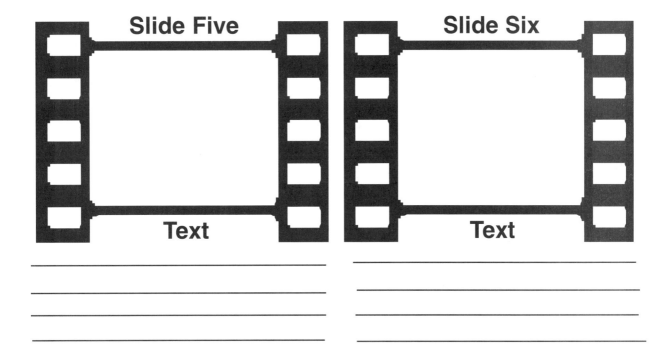

Slide Five

Text

_____

_____

_____

_____

Slide Six

Text

_____

_____

_____

_____

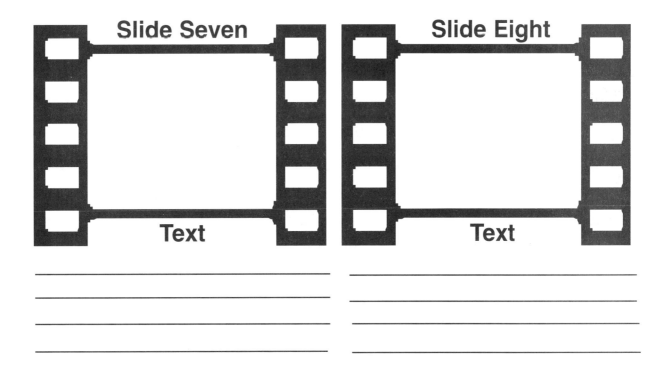

Slide Seven

Text

_____

_____

_____

_____

Slide Eight

Text

_____

_____

_____

_____

AN IMAGINARY PIZZA COMPANY TV COMMERCIAL ... HYPERSTUDIO STORYBOARD *(cont.)*

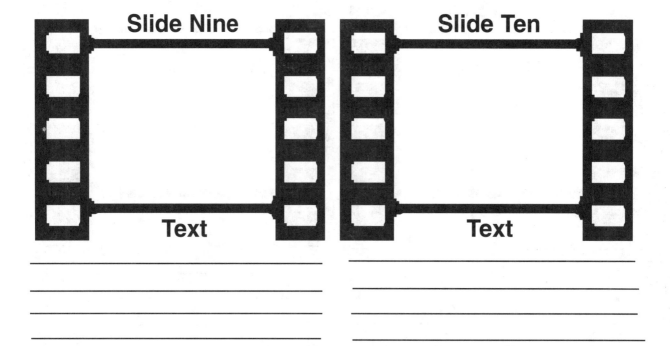

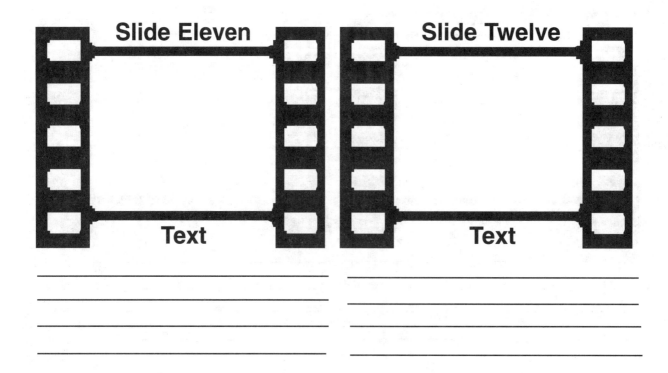

PIZZA VALUE CALCULATOR

	A	B	C	D	E	F	G	H
1	Pizza Restaurants							
2	Restaurant 1							
3	Cost	$8.99	$12.99	$16.99	$8.99	$12.99	$16.99	$18.99
4	Restaurant 2							
5	Cost	$9.19	$13.59	$17.49	$9.19	$13.59	$17.49	$21.10
6	Restaurant 3							
7	Cost	$8.49	$10.99	$18.84	$8.49	$10.99	$18.84	
8	Restaurant 4							
9	Cost	$9.99	$11.34	$17.09	$9.99	$11.34	$17.09	

1. Enter labels in Column A.

2. Enter pizza sizes in Row 1.

3. Enter the formulas for area in square inches in Row 2.

   Round = π x radius x radius

   Square = side x side

   Rectangle = length x width

4. Enter cost of pizzas.

5. Enter the formula for cost per square inch for each pizza restaurant:

   square inches of pizza/cost of pizza

Note: When students enter the cost of pizzas into this spreadsheet, it will calculate the cost of pizza per square inch. Students can use this data to determine the best pizza value based on the shape and size of the pizza. Then students can use local pizza ads to determine the best pizza value based on shape, size, and cost. This data can be used in the pizza party planning activity.

BEST PIZZA VALUE BASED ON PRICE PER SQUARE INCH SPREADSHEET AND CHART

	A	B	C	D	E	F	G	H
1	Pizza Restaurants							
2	Restaurant 1							
3	Value per square in.	$0.18	$0.11	$0.08	$0.14	$0.09	$0.07	$0.10
4	Restaurant 2							
5	Value per square in.	$0.18	$0.12	$0.09	$0.14	$0.09	$0.07	$0.11
6	Restaurant 3							
7	Value per square in.	$0.18	$0.10	$0.09	$0.13	$0.08	$0.07	$0.00
8	Restaurant 4							
9	Value per square in.	$0.20	$0.10	$0.09	$0.16	$0.08	$0.07	$0.00

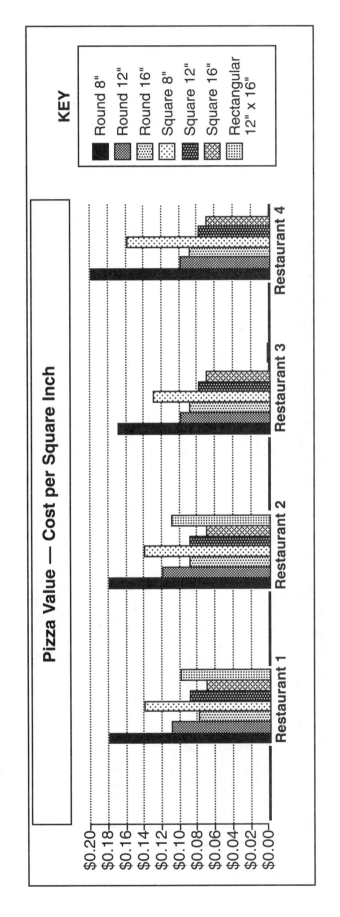

KEY

- Round 8"
- Round 12"
- Round 16"
- Square 8"
- Square 12"
- Square 16"
- Rectangular 12" x 16"

Pizza Value — Cost per Square Inch

BEST PIZZA VALUE BASED ON SIZE AND SHAPE SPREADSHEET AND CHART

Best Pizza Value Based on Size and Shape Spreadsheet and Chart

	A	B	C	D	E	F	G	H
1	Pizza Restaurants							
2	Restaurant 1							
3	Cost	$8.99	$12.99	$16.99	$8.99	$12.99	$16.99	$18.99
4	Restaurant 2							
5	Cost	$9.19	$13.59	$17.49	$9.19	$13.59	$17.49	$21.10
6	Restaurant 3							
7	Cost	$8.49	$10.99	$18.84	$8.49	$10.99	$18.84	
8	Restaurant 4							
9	Cost	$9.99	$11.34	$17.09	$9.99	$11.34	$17.09	

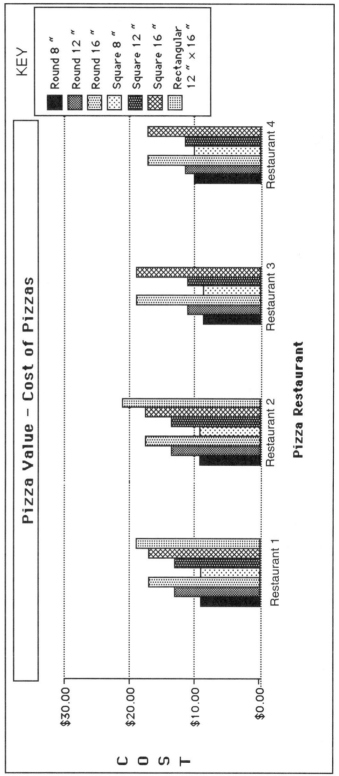

Pizza Value – Cost of Pizzas

KEY
- Round 8″
- Round 12″
- Round 16″
- Square 8″
- Square 12″
- Square 16″
- Rectangular 12″ × 16″

COST: $30.00, $20.00, $10.00, $0.00

Pizza Restaurant: Restaurant 1, Restaurant 2, Restaurant 3, Restaurant 4

PIZZA, COMPUTERS, AND KIDS ... A PIZZA RECIPE DATABASE

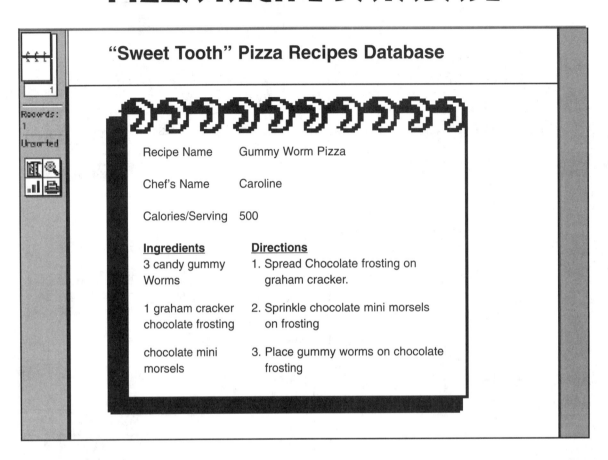

Directions

1. The teacher should create a database template with the following fields:

    Recipe Name
    Chef's Name
    Calories/Serving
    Ingredients

Directions

2. Have the students create "sweet tooth" pizza recipes and write them on the recipe planning sheet on pages 123–124.

3. Have the students calculate the approximate number of calories per serving by looking at the ingredient labels.

4. Have the students use the recipe planning sheet to enter data on the class "Sweet Tooth" Pizza Recipe Database.

5. Have the students sort data to answer questions about the "Sweet Tooth" Recipes Database. Page 126 has questions and can be duplicated for each student.

"SWEET TOOTH" PIZZA RECIPE PLANNING SHEET

RECIPE NAME _____

CHEF'S NAME _____

Calories Per Serving:

List the ingredients and number of calories below:

1. _____   _____

2. _____   _____

3. _____   _____

4. _____   _____

5. _____   _____

                              TOTAL   _____

Add the calories and put number on TOTAL line.

"SWEET TOOTH" PIZZA RECIPE
PLANNING SHEET, *(cont.)*

DIRECTIONS:

_____

_____

_____

_____

A sketch of my "Sweet Tooth" Pizza

PIZZA FLYER ... A DESKTOP PUBLISHING ACTIVITY

 # Pizza Works

Pizza Sale

Buy One Pizza
Get Second Pizza for 1/2 Price

Children Eat Free
(On Tuesdays)

"SWEET TOOTH" PIZZA RECIPE QUESTIONS

Name _____ Date _____

Quick Talk

Discuss what makes your pizza special with your group. Write down your thoughts.

_____

_____

Data Manipulation

1. Whose pizza has chocolate chips?

2. Whose pizza has red hots?

3. Whose pizza has coconut?

4. How many pizzas have chocolate frosting?

5. How many pizzas have vanilla frosting?

6. How many pizzas have M&M's?

7. How many pizzas have Gummy Bears?

8. Whose pizza has the same number of calories?

9. How many people have pizzas greater than 300 calories?

10. Who has a pizza most like yours? How are they alike?

Reflection

Write a sentence that describes your pizza.

_____

_____

PIZZA, COMPUTERS, AND KIDS ... A PIZZA NUTRITION DATABASE

Pizza Nutrition Database

Records:
1

Unsorted

Pizza Brand Name

Type of Pizza Pepperoni ▼

Ingredients

Calories/Serving

Protein

Carbohydrates

Total Fat

Calcium

Iron

Sodium

Directions

1. The teacher should create a database template with the following fields:

Pizza Brand Name	Type of Pizza
Total Fat	Calories/Serving
Sodium	Protein
Calcium	Iron
Ingredients	

2. Have the students go to a grocery store and find nutritional data about various brands of pizza. They can record this information on the data collection sheet on page 128.

3. Have the students enter this data into the Pizza Nutrition Database.

4. Have the students find, sort, and match the data to determine the most nutritious brand of pizza.

PIZZA NUTRITION DATA COLLECTION SHEET

Nutritional Value of Selected Brands of Pizza

Take this data collection sheet to a grocery store and record the nutritional value of six brands of pizza. This data will be used to create a database that will help you determine which brand of pizza has the best nutritional value.

	B	C	D	E	F	G	H	I
1	Type	Calories	Fat	Sodium	Protein	Calcium	Carbs	Iron
2								
3								
4								
5								
6								

I think that _____ brand of pizza is the most

nutritious because_____

_____

_____

_____

INTEGRATED LESSON PLAN

Date: _____ Student Grouping: _____ Curriculum Area: _____ Grade Level: _____

Activity Description: _____

Curriculum Objective(s)	Technology Objective(s)	Interpersonal Objective(s)	Standards

Resources/Materials:

ALTERNATIVE ASSESSMENTS

Written	Verbal	Kinesthetic	Visual
booklet	book report	role-play	banner
diary	comparison	demonstration	poster
list	interview	field trip	collage
poem	monologue	invention	mobile
story	rap	paper-mâché	model
picture dictionary	song	charade	painting
commercial	jingle	dramatization	puzzle
play	speech	finger puppets	sign
letter	commercial	mime	time line
comparison	dialogue	puppets	cartoon
word search	joke	singing	drawing
crossword puzzle	skit	dancing	mural
newspaper	story	experiment	map
news headlines	description	game	scrapbook
report	tape recording	musical	slide show
autobiography	tall tale	recipe	videotape
biography	musical	model	diorama
book report	characterization	videotape	chart/graph

COMPUTER JOURNAL TEMPLATE

WHAT I LEARNED ABOUT	WHAT I LEARNED TO DO ON THE COMPUTER
WHAT I LEARNED ABOUT GETTING ALONG WITH OTHERS	WHAT I LIKED ABOUT THIS PROJECT

HYPERSTUDIO STORYBOARD

Name: _____

Date: _____

Card 1

Card 2

Card 3

Card 4

Card 5

Card 6

Appendix

SLIDE SHOW STORYBOARD

Name: _____ Date: _____

Slide 1	**Slide 2**	**Slide 3**
Text	Text	Text
Slide 4	**Slide 5**	**Slide 6**
Text	Text	Text

© *Teacher Created Materials, Inc.* 133 *#2430 Integrating Technology into the Social Studies*

INTERNET RESOURCES DATABASE

The following are directions for creating a database that documents sources for text and graphics that have been taken from the Internet:

1. Open a new database application.

2. Define the following fields:
   - item
   - brief description of item
   - title of item
   - author
   - URL

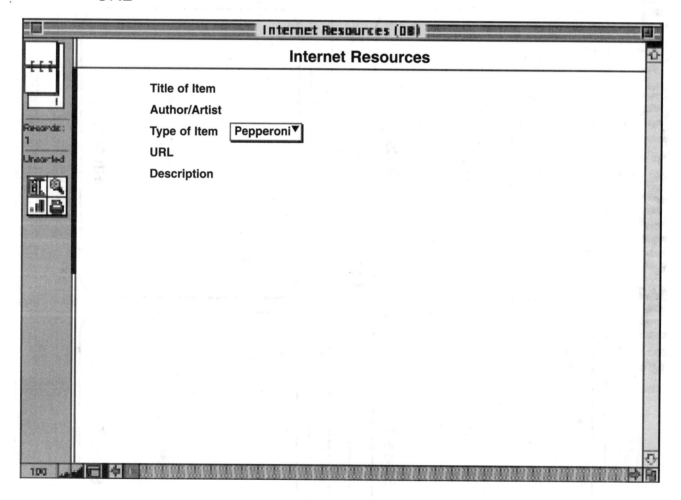

3. Save the database file as "Internet Resources."

4. Use this database to document the sources for the items that you take off the Internet.

LEARNING JOURNAL DATABASE

A Sample Learning Journal

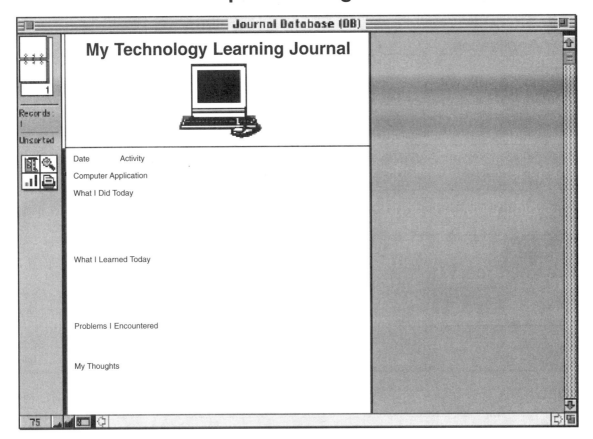

Directions

1. Open a new database file.

2. Define the following fields:
   - Date
   - Activity
   - Computer Application
   - What I Did Today
   - What I Learned Today
   - Problems I Encountered
   - My Thoughts

3. Go to the Layout mode to create layout.

4. Save the file as a stationery file (Macintosh) or template (IBM/PC).

5. Help students copy this file to their disks.

6. Students make entries each day in a new record.

7. Students enter information in the Browse mode.

MY TECHNOLOGY LEARNING JOURNAL

Date: _____   Activity _____

Computer Application _____

What I Did Today

_____

_____

_____

What I Learned Today

_____

_____

_____

Problems Encountered

_____

_____

_____

My Thoughts

_____

_____

_____

Appendix

DIRECTIONS FOR SELF-CHECKING SKILL SHEETS

1. Open a new spreadsheet document.

2. Change the columns and rows to the desired sizes.

3. Enter Question in column A.

4. Leave a space for the answer in column B and response in column C.

	A	B	C
1	**Question**	**Answer**	☑
2	UREOEP	EUROPE	WOW
3	IASA		
4	FICARA		
5	NRHMRCOTAEIA		
6	SRHMUCOTAEIA		
7	UTAIASRLA		
8	TCCANARTIA		

5. Enter the if-then formula for each cell.

=If B2="EUROPE","WOW!","SORRY!")

=If B3="ASIA","WOW!","SORRY!")

=If B4="AFRICA","WOW!","SORRY!")

=If B5="NORTHAMERICA","WOW!","SORRY!")

=If B6="SOUTHAMERICA","WOW!","SORRY!")

=If B7="AUSTRALIA","WOW!","SORRY!")

=If B8="ANTARCTICA","WOW!","SORRY!")

6. Save the file as a stationery file (Macintosh) or template (IBM/PC).

VENN DIAGRAM TEMPLATE

The following are directions for creating a Venn Diagram template that allows students to compare and contrast concepts and characteristics:

1. Open the drawing application.

2. Use the oval tool to draw two large overlapping circles.

3. Create individual text boxes for each circle: each concept or similarities and differences between concepts.

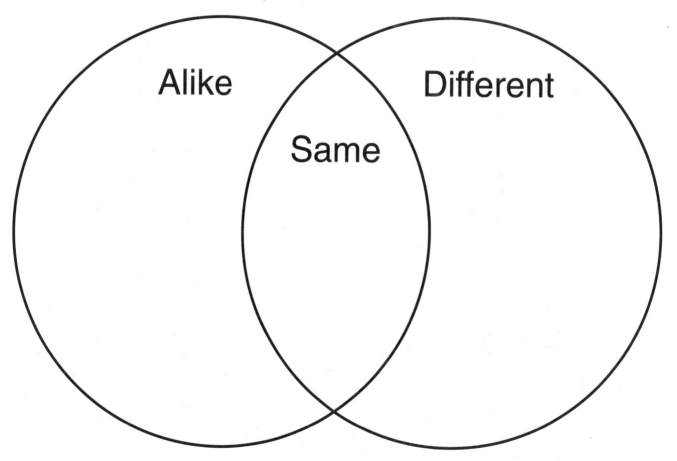

4. In the center where the circles overlap, place characteristics that the concepts have in common.

5. Label the diagram.

6. Change the colors, sizes, fonts, and styles of the text if desired.

7. Save the file as a stationery file (Macintosh) or a template (IBM/PC).

HOW TO CREATE STATIONERY FILES

There is a feature in *ClarisWorks* that allows you to save a document as a stationery file. Stationery is a special type of document that allows your original saved document to stay intact and gives you a copy of that document. You can add to or change the document and then save it with a different name. This feature allows you to make a document somewhat permanent and use it over and over again.

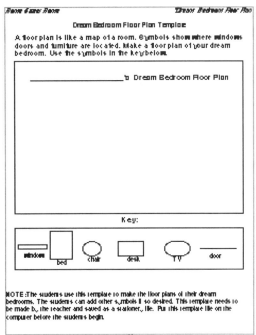

When you click on the stationery button in the save dialog box, the document is saved as is and cannot be altered and saved under the same name again. Let's look at the example of the Dream Bedroom Floor Plan Template from page 27. This document has been named Dream Bedroom Template and saved as a stationery file.

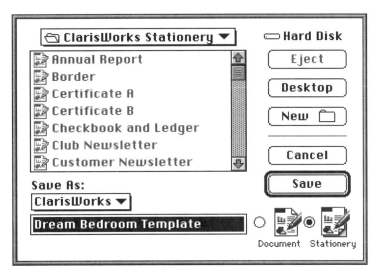

HOW TO CREATE STATIONERY FILES *(cont.)*

Students can use this document over and over again without changing it. A student can name this file " My Dream Bedroom" and save it to his or her disk. This file is a copy of the original document with the student's changes. The original document stays intact, ready to be opened by the next student.

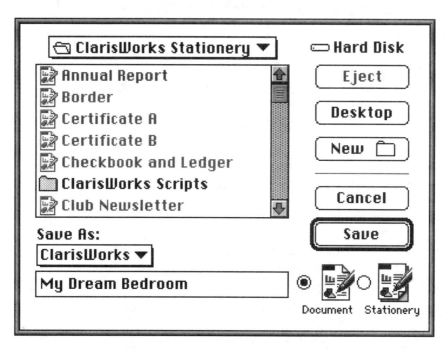

Students can access stationery files in the applications screen by clicking on the Use Assistant or Stationery box. When this box is clicked, the student can choose the Dream Bedroom Template and click on the OK button to open it.

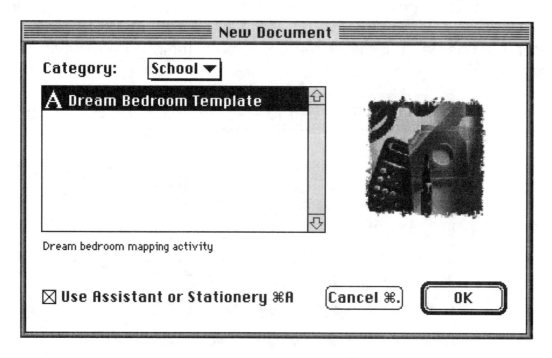

SAMPLE SOCIAL STUDIES PROJECT RUBRIC

Project has accurate detail and depth.

0 Incorrect facts, little detail

1 Some facts, some detail

2 Substantial facts, good amount of detail

3 Exceptional facts, vivid descriptions

Project has a clear focus.

0 Vague and unclear

1 Some focus, not well-organized

2 Well-organized, clear presentation

3 Very organized, easy to follow

Project demonstrates elements of design.

0 Little to no layout and design

1 Could be better organized

2 Attractive

3 Exceptional design, outstanding visual appeal

SOCIAL STUDIES INTERNET LINKS

- **Atlapedia**

  http://www.atlapedia.com/index.html

  Atlapedia Online contains key information on every country of the world.

  Each country profile provides facts and data on geography, climate, people, religion, language, history, and economy.

- **Classroom Connect**

  http://www.classroom.net/

  Database contains more than a thousand online links to high-quality educational sites as reviewed by the staff of Classroom Connect!

- **Harcourt Brace**

  http://www.hbschool.com/

  This resource provides subject-area activities designed to be done by individuals or by cooperative groups.

- **Culture Quest**

  http://www.ipl.org/youth/cquest/

  Join Parsifal the penguin and Olivia the owl as they explore different cultures. They sample delicious cuisines, play games, see museums full of arts, crafts, and history, hear folktales, and learn about holidays and festivals.

- **POTUS (Presidents of the United States)**

  http://www.ipl.org/ref/POTUS/

  This resource includes background information, election results, cabinet members' names and positions, presidency highlights, and some odd facts on each of the presidents with links to biographies, historical documents, audio and video files, and other presidential sites.

- **Architecture in Education**

  http://whyy.org/aie/page2.html

  This resource helps teachers integrate the study of architecture into their lesson plans through suggested activities and sample projects. It also connects teachers with each other, architects, and architectural students.

SOCIAL STUDIES INTERNET LINKS *(cont.)*

- **History/Social Studies Web Site for K-12 Teachers**

  http://www.execpc.com/~dboals.html

  This Web site provides K–12 classroom teachers help in locating and using history and social studies resources found on the Internet in the classroom.

- **Multicultural Calendar**

  http://www.kidlink.org:80/KIDPROJ/MCC/

  Multicultural calendar entries contain information about recipes for holiday foods, historical background, significance of the holidays, and the special ways in which these days are observed.

- **Kids Voting USA**

  http://kidsvotingusa.org/

  It allows students to visit official polling sites to cast a ballot similar in content to the official ballot.

- **NCSS Online Educators' Area**

  http://www.ncss.org/online/educators.html

  This National Council for the Social Studies site provides resources for social studies education, including news, professional development opportunities, information on meetings and seminars, and links to local and regional social studies organizations.

- **Lesson Plans and Resources for Social Studies Teachers**

  http://www.csun.edu/~hcedu013/index.html

  This resource provides lesson plans and resources from the Internet.

- **national geographic.com**

  http://www.nationalgeographic.com/main.html

  The National Geographic Society Web site provides resources for teachers and students.

- **Nebraska Department of Education Social Science Resources Home Page**

  http://www.nde.state.ne.us/SS/ss.html

  This home page includes a lesson plan search engine.

SOCIAL STUDIES INTERNET LINKS *(cont.)*

- **Web Sites and Resources for Teachers**

  http://www.csun.edu/~vceed009/index.html

  Sites and resources from the Internet are available for teachers to use in their classrooms. They range from lesson plans, creative classroom projects, interactive activities, visits to museums, and trips around the U.S.A. and other countries.

- **Houghton Mifflin's Social Studies Center**

  http://www.eduplace.com/ss/index.html

  Ideas enhance the teaching of social studies.

- **Social Studies Sources**

  http://education.indiana.edu/~socialst/

  Find social studies resources for K–12 social studies teachers and students.

- **The Learning Web**

  http://www.usgs.gov/education/

  This collection of educational resources can be used in the classroom to teach earth science concepts.

- **Keypals**

  http://www.keypals.com/p/keypals.html

  A keypal is a modern-day pen pal. Keypals allows you to connect with teachers and students from all over the world.

- **Kids Web**

  http://www.keypals.com/p/keypals.html

  Kids Web is a worldwide digital library for school kids. It has connections to hundreds of other sites for children.

- **Pitsco**

  http://www.pitsco.com/

  This Web site provides educators with innovative, exciting, and hand-on activities for their classrooms.

- **Kathy Schrock's Guide for Educators**

  http://www.capecod.net/schrockguide/

  This guide offers a classified list of sites on the Internet for the enhancement of curriculum and teacher professional growth.